TAYLOR SWIFT

Every Day Is a Fairytale

THE UNOFFICIAL STORY

LIV SPENCER

ECW Press

© ECW Press, 2010

Published by ECW Press
2120 Queen Street East, Suite 200, Toronto, Ontario, Canada M4E 1E2
416-694-3348 / info@ecwpress.com

LIBRARY AND ARCHIVES CANADA CATALOGUING IN PUBLICATION

Spencer, Liv
Taylor Swift : every day is a fairytale : the unofficial story / Liv Spencer.

ISBN 978-1-55022-931-8
also issued as 978-1-55490-931-5 (PDF) and 978-1-77090-167-4 (EPUB)

1. Swift, Taylor, 1989- —Juvenile literature. 2. Country
musicians—United States—Biography—Juvenile literature.
I. Title.

ML3930.S989S64 2010   J782.42164´092   C2009-905974-6

Text and photo editor: Crissy Boylan
Cover and interior design and typesetting: Tania Craan

*Thank you to the T-Swift fans who helped with photos of the Fearless Tour. Special thank you to Jennifer Knoch and Crissy
Boylan for their invaluable contributions to this book and for making sure I never never never give up! — Liv*

Second printing: November 2011 at United Graphics, Mattoon, IL, USA.

The publication of *Taylor Swift: Every Day Is a Fairytale, The Unofficial Story* has been generously
supported by the Ontario Arts Council, by the Government of Ontario through the Ontario Book Publishing
Tax Credit, by the OMDC Book Fund, an initiative of the Ontario Media Development Corporation, and by
the Government of Canada through the Canada Book Fund.

Canada   ONTARIO ARTS COUNCIL
CONSEIL DES ARTS DE L'ONTARIO

Table of Contents

Introduction

In the not-too-distant pop-music past, a superstar with multi-platinum-selling records, shelves full of awards, and a sold-out headlining tour seemed as remote to her millions of fans as a star in the night sky. Rarely communicating directly with her fans, interviews with the media and public appearances were a celebrity's way of keeping in touch. Even today some pop stars keep their distance. Not Taylor Swift. With her constant video diaries, blog posts, and tweets, Taylor is in nearly daily contact with the Taylor Nation, hugging fans at meet-and-greets before her concerts and sending them direct emails through her MySpace. Just like in the confessional-style lyrics she writes for her number-one hits, this platinum-haired and platinum-selling singer-songwriter isn't afraid to share her real self with the world. And that openness and honesty has been a crucial part of Taylor's huge success; it's easy to feel Taylor could be your best friend, one you admire for her relentless dedication and hard work.

Ever since she was a little girl in Pennsylvania listening to "uncool" country music, Taylor has fought to turn her life into the fairytale she imagined for herself. She sings about princesses and princes but never plays the helpless maiden; instead she chases her dreams and makes them reality. Here in *Taylor Swift: Every Day Is a Fairytale*, Taylor's journey is chronicled — her childhood, her loving and supportive family, her first attempts at getting a record deal as a precocious pre-teen, her songs, her videos, her friends, and her ever-growing list of accomplishments. What emerges is the picture of a young woman who never, never, never gives up — and has succeeded in writing her own fairytale.

Growing Up Swiftly

chapter 1

On December 13, 1989, the number-one song topping the charts was Billy Joel's baby-boomer anthem "We Didn't Start the Fire." Little did anyone know, in the small borough of Wyomissing, Pennsylvania, a spark was being born in the form of Taylor Alison Swift, who would burn up the charts less than two decades later.

Taylor's savvy parents — Andrea Swift, a successful businesswoman, and Scott Swift, a stockbroker — wanted to make sure their daughter would have every advantage possible, and named her appropriately. Andrea reasoned that future employers wouldn't know if Taylor was a boy or a girl if they saw her name on a business card or résumé. Taylor explained to *Rolling Stone*, "She wanted me to be a business person in a business world." The platinum-selling singer-songwriter may not work in a boardroom, but there's no doubt Andrea Swift is anything but disappointed.

In Wyomissing, Taylor grew up on an 11-acre Christmas tree farm, which was the family's secondary business. The farm was also home to several cats and seven horses. Taylor was a young equestrian, and rode horses competitively as a child. Taylor remembers, "I was raised on a little farm and for me when I was little, it was the biggest place in the world. And it was the most magical, wonderful place in the world." She spent her time "running free and going anywhere I wanted in my head." When she was two she got a partner to play with when Andrea and Scott brought brother Austin home to join the Swift family. When Taylor was four, Andrea decided to set her career aside and focus on her family.

As Taylor shared in "The Best Day," her love song for her family, the Swifts are a close-knit bunch. Telling *Girls' Life* about her mom, Taylor explained, "She's one of my best friends. She's always, always around. She's the person in my life who will just literally look me in the eye and say, 'Look, snap out of it.' You know? And I need that person." Taylor also recognizes that her mother's influence

was a major factor in achieving her astonishing success: "She totally raised me to be logical and practical. I was brought up with such a strong woman in my life and I think that had a lot to do with me not wanting to do anything halfway."

The special bond between mother and daughter doesn't go unnoticed by Scott Swift, who told the *Tennessean*: "People keep saying to me, 'The relationship between Andrea and Taylor is something pretty special.' That is amazing. There aren't too many mother and daughters who work together as a business unit the way those two do." And while Scott may not be constantly by Taylor's side now that she's often away from home, he still plays a major role in his daughter's life. Andrea's approach is firm though loving, realistic, and honest, while Scott is a softie. "My dad is just a big teddy bear who tells me that everything I do is perfect," said Taylor. Like his wife, Scott passes on his wisdom to his daughter, helping her make sound financial decisions about her career independently. "Business-wise, he's brilliant," says Taylor. "I'm constantly getting business advice and what to invest in. I think you should be in charge of every single aspect of your career."

As a parenting team, Andrea and Scott balance each other out. Taylor told the *Tennessean*, "I have a logical, practical, realistic mother, and a head-in-the-clouds, kind and friendly, optimistic father. And so I'm a dreamer, and my imagination goes to places where love lasts forever and everything is covered in glitter, and that's from my dad's personality. Every time I walk off stage, he tells me how much he loved it, or how he was standing at the soundboard, crying. But my mom, she'll tell me exactly what she saw."

While Taylor may get her confidence and her business sense from her parents, her musical talent comes from someone else: her late maternal grandmother, Marjorie Finlay, a successful opera singer. Taylor reminisces, "I can remember her singing, the thrill of it. She was one of my first inspirations," and she elaborated to the *Sunday Times*: "She would have these wonderful parties at her house, and she would get up and sing. She always wanted to be onstage, whether she was in the middle of her living room or in church; she just loved it. And when she would walk into a room, everyone would look at her, no matter what; she had this 'thing,' this It factor. I always noticed it — that she was different from everyone else." Marjorie traveled with her husband, who built oil rigs around the world, and she performed in places like Singapore, Puerto Rico, and Vietnam. When Andrea was 10, the family settled in America. Marjorie appeared in operas like *The Bartered Bride* and *The Barber of Seville* and musicals such as *West Side Story*. Scott Swift notices similarities that go beyond musical ability between his daughter and his mother-in-law: "The two of them had some sort of magic where they could walk into a room and remember everybody's name. Taylor has the grace and the same physique of Andrea's mother. Andrea's mother had this unique quality; if she was going into a room, literally everybody loved Marjorie."

Taylor's legacy from her grandmother appeared at a very young age. She had an uncanny ability to memorize songs, and Taylor remembers that at age three or four, "I

would come out of these Disney movies and I'd be singing every single song from the movie on the car ride home, word for word. And my parents noticed that once I had run out of words I would just make up my own." Taylor admits, "I was that annoying kid who ran around singing for random strangers."

The young girl was hooked on more than just singing; Taylor was addicted to stories too. Taylor told Katie Couric, "All I wanted to do was talk and all I wanted to do was hear stories. I would drive my mom insane driving down the road [with her]." Like other children, Taylor demanded stories at bedtime, but rather than reading the same books over and over, Taylor insisted on originals. "I refused to go to bed without a story. And I always wanted to hear a new one," she says. No wonder Andrea admitted her energetic youngster "had the potential to be exhausting."

It wasn't too long before Taylor started making up her own stories. She told the *Washington Post*, "Writing is pretty involuntary to me. I'm always writing." Taylor's love of language "started with poetry, trying to figure out the perfect combination of words, with the perfect amount of syllables and the perfect rhyme to make it completely pop off the page." She loved Dr. Seuss and Shel Silverstein, and told *Rolling Stone*: "I noticed early on that poetry was something that just stuck in my head and I was replaying those rhymes and try[ing] to think of my own. In English, the only thing I wanted to do was poetry and all the other kids were like, 'Oh, man. We have to write poems again?' and I would have a three-page long poem." In the fourth grade she won a national poetry contest for her composition

A young Taylor as Kim in a children's theater production of *Bye Bye Birdie*.

"Monster in My Closet." She even wrote a 350-page novel during a summer vacation. Andrea remembers, "She wrote all the time. If music hadn't worked out, I think she'd be going off to college to take journalism classes or trying to become a novelist."

Beyond music and stories, Taylor demonstrated one more quality at a young age that would prove useful on her rise to superstardom: she was at ease in front of the camera and knew how to strike a pose that even Tyra Banks would call fierce. Andrea told British magazine *Sugar*, "I got photos taken for family Christmas cards when Taylor was five. She was really posing. The photographer told me I should take her to L.A. to model, but I'm so glad I didn't." Millions of fans are glad she didn't too.

Entering the Spotlight

When Taylor was around 10, she decided she wanted to follow in her grandmother's footsteps and sing in front of an audience. She auditioned for the local children's theater company a week after she saw its production of *Charlie and the Chocolate Factory*. Since she was tall, Taylor was given the lead roles, and played such memorable parts as Sandy in *Grease*, Kim in *Bye Bye Birdie*, and Maria in *The Sound of Music*, but Taylor admits, "My singing sounded a lot more country than

quent karaoke contests. Taylor started going every week, taking her parents along with her. "They were kind of embarrassed by it, I guess," remembered Taylor. "This little girl singing in this smoky bar. But they knew how much it meant to me so they went along with it." A year and a half later, her performance of LeAnn Rimes' "Big Deal" earned her not only the prestige of being karaoke champion, but also a spot opening for Grammy-winner and country legend Charlie Daniels at the amphitheater across the street. In this case, "opening" meant that Taylor went on at 10 a.m. while Charlie Daniels played at 8 p.m. Nevertheless, it was a pretty amazing feat for an 11-year-old.

Demonstrating business smarts that would make her parents proud, Taylor discovered that another way to reach a large audience was to perform the national anthem at sports games. She sent demo tapes out everywhere. She sang regularly for her local minor league baseball team, the Reading Phillies, and would take whatever other gigs she could get from local garden club meetings all the way up to the U.S. Open tennis tournament when she was 12. "I figured out that if you could sing that one song, you could get in front of 20,000 people without even having a record deal," Taylor told *Rolling Stone*. One of the highlights of her anthem-singing career came at age 11 when she sang at a 76ers game. Jay-Z was sitting courtside and, after her performance, the famous rapper and hip hop mogul gave young T-Swizzle a high-five. "I bragged about that for like a year straight," Taylor admits.

As her career progressed, Taylor kept singing the anthem, though her eventual

Broadway." And though Taylor liked being onstage, what really captured her heart was performing karaoke at the cast parties. The songstress explains, "Singing country music on that karaoke machine was my favorite thing in the world." She sang the Shania Twain, Dixie Chicks, and Faith Hill songs that she'd been listening to since a LeAnn Rimes album got her hooked on country music at age six. Her inspiring performances didn't go unnoticed, and Taylor remembers, "One day, somebody turned to my mom and said, 'You know, she really ought to be singing country music.'" Taylor adds, "It kind of occurred to all of us at the same time that that's what I needed to be doing."

Taylor started scouring the phone book for more places to perform. One of her regular spots was the Pat Garrett Roadhouse in Strausstown, Pennsylvania, which held fre-

record deal helped get her in front of considerably larger audiences. She performed "The Star-Spangled Banner" at game three of the 2008 World Series between the Philadelphia Phillies and the Tampa Bay Rays. Even though she'd sung the anthem hundreds of times, performing at such an important game was still a little daunting. Taylor explained, "The national anthem is not as challenging range-wise, because I've been doing it for so long. The challenge for me is the utter silence that comes over 40,000 people in a baseball stadium and you're the only one singing it. . . . It's a really surreal moment for me."

But before she was a household name performing at one of the nation's most important sporting events, Taylor was just trying to find an audience. She watched a TV special about one of her heroes, Faith Hill, who talked about making it in Nashville, the home of country music. Taylor realized, "That's the promised land for country music. That's where I need to go."

Taylor made a demo tape of her singing the country songs she had grown to love backed by karaoke tracks, and convinced her mom to take her to the legendary city on a spring break trip. Andrea packed up Taylor and Austin and they drove down to Nashville. Taylor walked into the record-company offices on Music Row, handed them her demo, and boldly announced, "Hi, I'm Taylor. I'm 11. I really want a record deal." But as charming as the aspiring star's courage was, the companies weren't wooed. "Basically all the record companies went, 'Ah, how cute. She's just a little kid.' [and] 'Give up your dreams. Go home and come back when you're 18,'" recalls Taylor. "I chose not to hear that. I wasn't prepared to accept that I wasn't a relevant artist until I was 18." The record companies steadfastly believed that young people didn't listen to country music. Taylor was frequently told, "The country music demographic is 35-year-old females and those are the only people who listen to country music," but she remembers, "I just kept thinking that can't be true. That can't be accurate because I listen to country music and I know there have to be other girls everywhere who listen to country music. . . . So I kept trying because I didn't believe that there was just one tiny demographic." Of course, that younger demographic *did* exist, and while the record execs might not have known it yet, Taylor did, and in a few short years, she would prove it to them.

Guitar Hero, Social Outcast

Returning home to Wyomissing, Taylor knew she had to do something to distinguish herself from all the other wannabe performers, and she came up with two ways she could do that: she'd learn to play the guitar and she'd write her own music. Taylor explained, "There are a lot of gorgeous voices and beautiful women in Nashville, so I had to figure out a way to stand out. I thought if I could walk into an audition and play a song that I had written, then I'd stand out. And that has really made a difference."

Taylor had a guitar already — she'd received an electric guitar at age eight, and had actually started taking lessons but she had been discouraged quickly. It was a less formal teacher who got her playing for good; she

learned her first three chords from a guy who came by to fix the family's computer. Ten minutes later, she'd written her first song, "Lucky You." Each week, the computer guy would teach his young pupil a few more chords. By age 12, she was playing guitar four hours a day, every day. In classic T-Swift style, she decided to play on the more challenging 12-string model, as opposed to a six-string, because her first teacher had told her she wouldn't be able to do it. She told *Teen Vogue*, "I actually learned on a 12-string, purely because some guy told me that I'd never be able to play it, that my fingers were too small. Anytime someone tells me that I can't do something, I want to do it more." Andrea was floored by her daughter's commitment: "Her fingers would crack from so much playing. She was driven beyond anything I had ever witnessed."

Taylor's single-minded commitment to music may have wowed her mother, but it wasn't something that made her popular at school. The other kids made fun of her bleeding fingers and her love for country music, and were jealous of the attention she received for performing. She remembers, "I kind of started to live in fear when I would sing the national anthem at the 76ers game. If there was a write-up about it the next day in our local paper, I knew it was gonna be a bad day at school for me." A group of popular girls who used to be friendly with Taylor decided to exclude her: "When I'd sit down at the lunch table, they'd get up and move. Or, as I was setting up my equipment to sing karaoke at the town summer festival, the kids would shout horrible things." Andrea recalls, "She was shunned. After school, I'd hear what nightmare had occurred that day,

what awful thing was done to her. I'd have to pick her up off the floor."

The budding performer also found her priorities were hugely different from those of her classmates: "All the girls at school were going to sleepovers and breaking into their parents' liquor cabinets on the weekend, and all I wanted to do was go to festivals and sing karaoke music." Taylor still picks music over drinking and parties, and since making that decision in junior high, the songstress has retained the same values — she won't let anything compromise her music career.

Despite rejecting the more rebellious aspects of the social scene, the outsider still desperately wanted to fit in, and Taylor tried to act just like everyone else. She even attempted to tame her curly locks, imitating the straight-haired look of the popular girls. "I tried so hard to be like everybody else and do what they did and like the things they liked," she said. "I tried so hard and it didn't work. They still didn't want to be friends with me. . . . So I found that trying to be like everyone else doesn't work." Looking back, Taylor can see what drove her need to conform: insecurity. "Whatever makes you different in middle school makes you uncool somehow. I hate that. I think that one thing I realized, after the fact, was that everybody was insecure. Maybe it wasn't the same insecurity that I had, but it's always something. It's funny how after you get out of middle school, the thing that you were the most insecure about can be the thing that sets you apart." With the wisdom of a few more years and a wildly successful career, Taylor offered comfort to other teens who may be going through the same thing, saying, "The only place where it's cool to be the same as everyone else is junior high." Trapped in her school's hallways, Taylor eventually came to terms with the fact that she'd never be in-crowd material, and embraced what made her special, even if that meant standing out, and ultimately, standing apart from everyone else.

The straight-A student found herself in a lonely position on the outside, observing rather than joining in the regular goings-on of middle school. She recalls, "I was facing a lot of things at school where I found myself on the outside looking in. I was not included. I would go to school some days, a lot of days, and not know who I was going to talk to. And that's a really terrifying thing for somebody who's 12." Luckily, Taylor had an outlet for feeling alone and excluded; she channeled it into her songwriting. She wrote the song "The Outside" when she was 12 to capture that feeling, writing, "Nobody ever lets me in / I can still see you, this ain't the best view / On the outside looking in." Her point of view as an outsider became a great source of material for Taylor's songs: "The people around me provided all the inspiration I needed. Everything I wrote [at that time] came from that experience, what I observed happening around me."

Later in her career, Taylor would learn to be grateful to the people who had made her life so miserable and given her so much fuel for her songwriting. She realized, "The only thing I can do is look back and thank [those classmates]. If I hadn't been so driven to music because I didn't have anyone to hang out with, if I hadn't written songs because I didn't have anyone to talk to, I wouldn't be

sitting here right now."

But at the time, hurting from rejection and loneliness, she channeled everything into her music; writing songs became like a diary for Taylor, and it still is. As her mother told the *New York Times*, "She simply has to write songs. It's how she filters her life." Taylor was able to turn her schoolyard rejection into something bigger, something that brought her closer to her goal of having a record deal. Despite being a dreamer, Taylor knew achieving her goal wouldn't be easy, and that she had to keep writing, practicing, and performing to make it happen. Part of this practicality came from her mother, who, Taylor explains, "never said to me, 'Taylor, you're gonna be famous someday.'" Taylor continues, "There are so many moms who tell their kids that. But my mom has always been practical. She didn't know if I would succeed. She'd say, 'If you want a chance at this, you've got to work real-ly, really hard.'" And so Taylor did, writing and practicing constantly and performing at all the music festivals, karaoke competitions, and national-anthem gigs she could fit in around her school schedule. Taylor told *Cosmo Girl*, "The reason I was so driven was that I didn't expect that anything would just happen for me. But that doubt fueled me to work harder. My attitude was the opposite of people who are like, 'It's gonna happen for me. It's gonna happen for me.' My mantra was always 'It's not gonna happen for me. Go out and play the show or it won't happen.'"

One such show made a huge difference in Taylor's career — the U.S. Open, one of the four most prestigious tennis tournaments in the world. Taylor belted out "The Star-Spangled

Banner" in front of a massive crowd of over 20,000 tennis fans. Among them was Dan Dymtrow, then manager of Britney Spears. Impressed with Taylor's talent, Dymtrow took her on as a client and worked to promote the young artist. Dymtrow helped 13-year-old Taylor get a development deal with RCA Records in Nashville. It seemed like a huge step forward, but after holding onto her for a year, Taylor's contract came up for review. Taylor performed for RCA bigwigs, and the label decided to shelve her rather than have her make a record immediately. "That means they want to watch you, but they're not promising to make an album with you," explained Taylor. "Kind of like a guy who wants to date you but not be your boyfriend." It wasn't enough for the ambitious teen, who was in a hurry to share her music with the world. "I genuinely felt that I was running out of time. I'd written all these songs and I wanted to capture these years of my life on an album while they still represented what I was going through." But more than anything, Taylor was disappointed that RCA didn't have faith in her potential, so she walked away from the deal — a bold move for a young singer without a fallback plan. She recalls, "I figured if they didn't believe in me then, they weren't ever going to believe in me."

Taylor still believed in herself, and she worked at convincing her family to make a permanent move to the heartland of country music — Nashville, Tennessee. Her persistence paid off, and before Taylor's freshmen year the entire Swift family moved south for a fresh start in Music City, USA.

Next Stop, Nashville

chapter 2

Leaving Pennsylvania behind wasn't too difficult for Taylor, who was literally moving closer to her Nashville dream and away from her bullying classmates, but it required a bigger sacrifice from the rest of her uprooted family, especially her father, who had to transfer his business. Nevertheless, the Swifts never put pressure on Taylor. She told *Self* magazine, "I knew I was the reason they were moving. But they tried to put no pressure on me. They were like, 'Well, we need a change of scenery anyway' and 'I love how friendly people in Tennessee are.'" Andrea had faith in her daughter and trusted her intentions, "It was never about 'I want to be famous.' Taylor never uttered those words. It was about moving to a place where she could write with people she could learn from."

Taylor was glad her family trusted her instincts. "Sometimes you don't have a sure answer as to where you're going to go or where you're going to end up, but if you have an instinct as to where you don't need to be, you need to follow it and my parents let me make that decision completely," recalls Taylor.

She didn't have a label anymore, but she had experience working with one. In 2004, Taylor was featured in an Abercrombie & Fitch "rising stars" campaign and one of her songs appeared on a compilation album, the Maybelline-produced *Chicks with Attitude*. "The Outside," the song she'd written about feeling excluded in middle school, had found a temporary home.

It wasn't long before Taylor found a home as a songwriter at Sony/ATV Records. She was the youngest songwriter they'd ever hired, which is an impressive feat, but Taylor knew she'd still have to prove herself by acting with maturity beyond her years. "I knew the stereotype people had when they heard the words '14-year-old girl' was that I wasn't going to do the hard work, and I wanted people to know that I was," Taylor emphasized. "One of my first songwriting sessions was with [accomplished songwriter and producer] Brett Beavers, and I walked in with 15 different starts to songs. I love being prepared and I love organization, and I need people to know that I care and that this is important to me."

Being a professional songwriter meant that Taylor had to lead a sort of double life, going to high school in Hendersonville during the day and writing songs in the afternoons in downtown Nashville, less than 20 miles away. Taylor called her life back then "a really weird existence," and elaborated, "I was a teenager during the day when I was at school, and then at night it was like I was 45. My mom would pick me up from school and I'd go downtown and sit and write songs with these hit songwriters."

The social politics of high school in Tennessee turned out to be very similar to those of junior high in Pennsylvania, but luckily for Taylor, there was one major difference that made school tolerable — a great friend. Taylor met red-haired Abigail Anderson in ninth grade English, when the new girl wowed the class with her sophisticated composition. "We were the ones in the back of the class saying negative things about *Romeo and Juliet* because we were so bitter toward that emotion at the time," recalled Abigail. Neither girl was a member of the popular clique, so the pair made their own rules, focusing on

WELCOME TO MUSIC CITY, USA

With her songwriting gig, Taylor was part of the rich music history of Nashville, a city that has been home to music publishing since 1824 when *Western Harmony*, a book of hymns, was produced there. It was in the 1920s that Nashville music really began to flourish with the opening of the Grand Ole Opry. In the '40s and '50s, "Music Row" developed as Capitol Records and RCA first opened outposts in the capital and every other major label followed suit. Today, Nashville's 16th and 17th Avenues South are home to recording studios and labels galore.

The "Nashville Sound," a blend of a pop music sensibility with the traditional storytelling of folk and country artists, was popularized in the 1950s by legends like Jim Reeves, Patsy Cline, and Eddy Arnold. Its legacy can be heard in Taylor's song-crafting style that mixes infectious melodies with memorable tales rooted in real-life experiences.

As Nashville recording artist Elvis Presley helped make rock 'n' roll a craze, sales of country music albums dropped, and "crossing over" from country to mainstream listeners became hugely important for country artists. In the 1980s, the star of country crossover was the Queen of Country Music herself, Dolly Parton, whose music and personality made her a household name from coast to coast. Alongside the queen was the King of Country, George Strait, who trails only the Beatles and Elvis Presley for the number of hit albums he's released; he holds the record for the most number-one singles of any artist in any genre at 57, and he's always stayed true to a traditional honky-tonk sound. The '80s also saw the rise of hugely successful country acts such as Alabama and Reba McEntire.

Like a certain blonde teenager would 20 years later, Garth Brooks started as a Nashville songwriter before rapidly taking country music by storm with songs like "The Thunder Rolls" in the 1990s, bringing with him the "new country" sound, over 36 top 10 hits, record-breaking tours, and millions of albums sold. Garth's audience stretched well beyond the traditional country music boundaries. It's no surprise that Taylor Swift has called Garth Brooks her "role model."

But it was the female country musicians of the '90s that most influenced young Taylor, and it all started with then-14-year-old LeAnn Rimes' 1996 album *Blue*, which Taylor heard when she was just six years old. Recalls Taylor, "LeAnn Rimes was my first impression of country music . . . I just really loved how she could be making music and having a career at such a young age." Taylor "started listening to female country artists nonstop" from legends like Patsy Cline, Loretta Lynn, Tammy Wynette, and Dolly Parton to the stars of the '90s like Shania Twain, Faith Hill, and the Dixie Chicks. As Taylor explained to *Rolling Stone*, "I saw that Shania Twain brought this independence and this crossover appeal; I saw that

Dolly Parton, Tim McGraw, and Faith Hill at the 2000 ACM Award nominations. Taylor loves Dolly's response to male fans who interrupt quiet performance moments: "Some guy screamed from the crowd, 'I love you, Dolly!' and she goes, 'I thought I told you to stay in the truck!'"

Faith Hill brought this classic old-school glamour and beauty and grace; and I saw that the Dixie Chicks brought this complete 'we don't care what you think' quirkiness, and I loved what these women were able to do and what they were able to bring to country music."

Taylor has measured her career's progress by following in the footsteps of the legends who sang the music she grew up listening to. At a Bakersville, California, show shortly after Taylor's first album came out, the son of the late country legend Buck Owens presented her with a guitar: "I was on stage in front of 5,000 people and Buck Owens' son came out on stage with the red-white-and-blue guitar. Buck used to give them to [musicians] that he really respected, and [his son] said that this was the first one they had given away since we lost Buck. It blew my mind. I got really, really emotional. It was just so different than any other sort of respect. It was being approved and embraced by a country legend."

Another early career milestone for Taylor was the opportunity to play a show at the historic Grand Ole Opry. GAC filmed the experience (it's included on the deluxe version of her self-titled album). Taylor recounted, "There's this circle in the middle of the stage. It's like everybody from Patsy Cline to Keith Urban to LeAnn Rimes to me, now, have stood in this circle." At that moment, walking in the footsteps of country music's greats, Taylor knew she'd made it.

what they actually cared about rather than what other people did. For Taylor, that was music; for Abigail, competitive swimming: "When I was a freshman, I knew I wanted to swim in college, at a Division 1 school, and she knew that she wanted to go on tour." Such focus set the girls apart from their classmates, and bonded them together. Taylor explained to the *New York Times*, "It just dawned on me that I had to love being different or else I was going to end up being dark and angry and frustrated by school." Being different meant staying away from the popular-girl party scene, which Taylor had already decided didn't appeal to her. Taylor told *Glamour*, "I remember seeing girls crying in the bathroom every Monday about what they did at a party that weekend. I never wanted to be that girl."

Music & Lyrics

Now that she was in the home of country music and had a songwriting contract, Taylor didn't abandon her earlier confessional style to start writing about stereotypical country music subjects. "I don't sing about tractors and hay bales and things like that because that's not really the way that I grew up. But I do sing about the lessons I've learned," Taylor explained. She wanted to write for people her age, those country-music fans the labels told her didn't exist but she knew did — they were just waiting for songs they could relate to. "I don't try to write for older than I am and I don't try and write for younger than I am. I write in real time," noted the songwriter.

These real-time songs are, above all, personal and honest. They're about Taylor's feelings, her friends, her dreams, her heartbreak. She told *Seventeen*, "Honesty is a big part of my writing, because when I was younger and fell in love with songs I'd hear, I would always wonder who that song was about. It would totally have broken my heart to know it wasn't about anyone and was just written so it could be on the radio."

Now that she was at Hendersonville High, Taylor was accumulating all kinds of new material. She had her first flirtations with romance, and Taylor started to write the songs she'd become most famous for — songs about boys, love, and heartbreak. Since she is unafraid to name names, some of Taylor's early boyfriends are well known to her fans. These songs were a way for her to process her feelings and sometimes she directly addressed the person who inspired her words: "The only thing I think about when I'm writing a song is the person I'm writing the song about. Music is very confessional to me. It's a chance for me to say things I wouldn't be brave enough to say to the person's face."

Taylor's songs may be specific, but as millions of fans can attest, that doesn't mean they're not relatable. At first this came as a surprise to the young songwriter, who remembers, "I thought because my songs were so personal that nobody would be able to relate to them. . . . But apparently they were more significant to more people than just me." As it turns out, though the names may be different, the experiences Taylor writes about are fairly universal. Taylor reasoned, "The hardest thing about heartbreak is feeling like you're alone, and that the other person doesn't really care. But when you hear a song about it, you realize you're not alone — because the person who wrote it went through the same thing. That's what makes songs about heartbreak so relatable."

Because her inspiration came from immediate feelings and emotions, Taylor learned to write anytime and anywhere, not just in her after-school sessions at Sony. Stuck in class, she'd escape to the bathroom to record a melody on her cell phone, or scribble down lyrics alongside her lecture notes! Taylor admits, "When teachers conducted random notebook checks they'd be freaked out — but they learned to deal with me." If inspiration came outside of class, she'd use anything at hand to capture the words before she lost them. "I've seen her pull out a Kleenex and write a song on it," Abigail revealed.

Taylor doesn't write all her songs single-handedly. In fact, in those early Nashville days she met one very important collaborator: Liz Rose. Liz started in the industry with her own music publishing company, which she sold in 2001 to focus more seriously on her writing. It turned out to be a great career choice. Since then she's penned hits sung by country stars such as Trisha Yearwood, Bonnie Raitt, Tim McGraw, and Kellie Pickler. But Liz's collaboration with Taylor would prove to be her most prolific and successful. When the pair met, Liz instantly saw something exceptional in Taylor: "Even then, you knew she was going to do something. She was so driven and so talented."

Many fruitful songwriting sessions followed; Liz shares the writing credit on seven

Taylor embraces Liz Rose as they collect a Grammy for Best Country Song on January 31, 2010.

songs on Taylor's self-titled debut album and four on *Fearless*. She helped write hits like "You Belong with Me," "Teardrops on My Guitar," and "White Horse." Liz humbly gives most of the credit to her young protégé: "My sessions with Taylor were some of the easiest I've ever done. Basically, I was just her editor. She'd write about what happened to her in school that day. She had such a clear vision of what she was trying to say. And she'd come in with some of the most incredible hooks." The elder songwriter elaborates, "She's a genius, coming in with ideas and a melody. She'd come in and write with this old lady and I never second-guessed her. I respect her a lot."

As Taylor was writing up a storm, she also recorded demos with a producer, Nathan Chapman, who was also just starting his career and was working in "a shack behind the publishing company," according to Taylor. She knew that Nathan was the right producer for her music, saying "I just fell in love with what he did with my songs." Like her collaboration with Liz Rose, Taylor's partnership with Nathan would continue through her career, and she would take the new producer with her on her rise to the top.

Songbird at the Bluebird

With hundreds of hours of guitar playing and songwriting under her belt, Taylor was looking for a chance to show off her talents to the country music elite, and it came in the form of a showcase at Nashville's famous Bluebird Café. The café auditions performers for songwriters' nights, and those who are very successful can be booked for a showcase night, an event that draws local industry professionals hunting for new talent. A major country star had gotten his big break at the Bluebird — in 1987 a young Garth Brooks was discovered there and signed by Capitol Records after a showcase performance.

On Taylor's night to shine, she took the stage and played an acoustic set, and when she looked out at the audience, she noticed one person who was completely absorbed in the music, listening with his eyes closed to take it all in. "He was listening better than anyone in the room," remembers Taylor. That person was Scott Borchetta, a former executive at a Nashville division of Universal Music Group, who Taylor had met once before, playing a few songs for the exec before he left his DreamWorks Nashville office. "I was just smitten on the spot. It was like a lightening bolt," he told Great American Country.

After the show, Scott approached Taylor, and told her, "I have good news and I have bad news. . . . The good news is that I want to sign you to a record deal. The bad news is that I'm no longer with Universal Records." But Scott Borchetta had a plan for his own label and told the young songwriter, "I want you to wait for me . . . I'm working on something." Taylor remembers, "The way he said it convinced me that there was something going on that I wanted to be a part of."

An essential part of their deal was that Taylor would get to write all the songs that would appear on her albums. A larger label might have forced her to record tracks penned by other songwriters, but Taylor refused to compromise on what had been the foundation of her career. She told the *Sunday Times*, "It

A SHORT HISTORY OF BIG MACHINE RECORDS

Scott Borchetta got his first taste of the music business at a young age, working in the mailroom of his father's independent promotion company. He also approached music hands on, playing various instruments in several bands. But rather than trying to get his name in lights, Scott decided to help other people reach musical stardom. He worked for several labels including Mary Tyler Moore's MTM Records and MCA Records, and launched DreamWorks Nashville, which was part of Universal Music Group before the division shut down in 2005.

Scott started Big Machine Records in September of that year, and the company had its first number-one single, Jack Ingram's "Wherever You Are," eight months later. His early roster included Dusty Drake, Jack Ingram, Danielle Peck, Jimmy Wayne, and, of course, Taylor Swift. Though he jokes that when he told industry colleagues about his new 16-year-old sensation, "People would look at me cross-eyed. I would feel like they were deleting me from their BlackBerrys as I was telling them," he knew Taylor was a real talent. In 2006, he told *Billboard*, "I've had the good fortune of breaking everybody from Trisha Yearwood all the way up to Sugarland with big stops in between. This feels as big as any of them."

Since it opened its doors in 2005, Big Machine has expanded steadily, and in 2007, the CEO announced a new branch of Big Machine, Valory Music Group. The new division launched famed singer-songwriter Jewel's first country album, the debut album of *Billboard*'s "New Country Artist of 2009" Justin Moore, and represents Reba McEntire. In addition to Big Machine being distributed by Universal, Scott further re-established his connections with the major label in 2009 with a shared imprint, Republic Records Nashville, which represents acts such as The Band Perry and Sunny Sweeney. So how does Scott select who will become part of the Big Machine family? "I either fall in love with an artist's music or I don't," he explains. Good thing it was a love story with Taylor Swift's songs from day one.

Taylor with LeAnn Rimes, the singer who first got her interested in country music. Says Taylor: "Country music is the place to find reality in music, and reality in the stars who make that music. There's kindness and goodness and . . . honesty in the people I look up to, and knowing that makes me smile. I'm proud to sing country music, and that has never wavered."

would have really taken a lot of the wind out of my sails, personally, if I had to sing words that other people wrote; that would have killed me." Scott Borchetta's faith in her and the independence he promised her were enough to seal the deal . . . even if his company didn't yet exist. "Obviously, creative control is the most important thing for me, or I wouldn't have left the biggest label in Nashville for a label that didn't have any furniture," joked Taylor.

With a star-in-the-making like Taylor signed on, Scott now had even more motivation to get the new label up and running. He knew he had found someone incredibly special: "I was just killed on sight. She's the full package, somebody who writes her own songs, and is so good at it, so smart; who sings, plays the guitar, looks as good as she looks, works that hard, is that engaging and so savvy. It's an extraordinary combination."

Tryin' to Find a Place in This World

chapter 3

Scott Borchetta, Taylor, and Nathan Chapman, triumphant at the 2009 CMAs. Only three years earlier Taylor was in the studio with Nathan and Scott recording *Taylor Swift*.

With the support of Scott Borchetta and Big Machine Records, it was time for Taylor to start working on her first album. She entered the studio with Nathan Chapman, her demo producer, to record the tracks that would become her self-titled debut. Just like with Taylor's collaboration with Liz, she came to the studio with a definite idea of what her songs should sound like and Nathan's role as a producer was to translate those ideas into sonic perfection. She explained, "When I write a song I hear it completely produced in my head. I know exactly where I want the hook to be and I know what instruments I want to use. One of my favorite things to do is to sit around and obsess about how my music is going to sound. A lot of that goes on in the days following me writing a song. I will bring it into the studio with my producer Nathan, who I met when I was 14, and I will sing him the hook. We'll decide what we want to be playing on that. We've got it down to where we can understand each other before we even have to make much sense."

Over their many years of collaboration, Nathan has learned to trust Taylor's instincts: "Taylor knows just who she is. And she knows what she wants to say with the lyrics of her songs and with the music. She knows who she wants to be and where she fits in this big thing called the music business."

Though recording can be nerve-wracking for some new artists, Taylor wasn't intimidated by it, and saw it as a new extension of her dedication to music. She told GAC, "I love the recording process because I love singing, and it really gives me a chance to hone in on every single word — make it count, make it perfect." Ever the perfectionist, the process doesn't end for Taylor once her day in the recording booth does. She explained, "I leave the studio but I don't put it down. I don't stop listening and I don't stop tweaking and critiquing."

The tracks for the album were whittled down from a list of 40 songs to 11. When it came time to choose her first single, one song stood out for Scott Borchetta. Taylor had written it for a high school sweetheart, and she called it "When You Think Tim McGraw." Scott told *Dateline*, "She finished the song and I said, 'Do you realize what you just have written? Do you have any idea?' That was that moment of 'Oh my God.' And the grenade dropped in the still pond." The song's name was eventually shortened to "Tim McGraw," since that's how everyone referred to it. A quick session with Liz Rose at the piano perfected the song, Taylor recorded it, and her first single was released on June 19, 2006.

Over the next six months, "Tim McGraw" became almost as popular as its namesake: it hit number six on the Billboard Hot Country Songs chart and number 40 on the Hot 100 chart. Before the song hit the charts, Taylor got instant gratification when she was out for a drive and she heard her song requested on the radio for the first time. "I was, like, freaking out. I almost drove off the road," she told GAC.

When "Tim McGraw" was released, Taylor was finishing up her sophomore year at Hendersonville High. With her career taking off, a difficult decision had to be made: could she continue attending regular high school? She knew she wouldn't be able to dedicate herself 100% to her career if she had to keep a high-school timetable, so Taylor made the decision to homeschool. Abigail remembers, "She called me one night and we had to have the talk about she's not coming back to school . . . we dealt with it, and we've actually gotten closer since." It was a hard transition for both girls. Said Abigail, "She had to do her own thing out there and miss everything that had been her life for the previous few years.

that his granddaughter was a big fan of Taylor's and that she was getting straight As. Scott thought this was just typical grandfatherly pride until the man added, "She wasn't getting straight As, but she heard Taylor Swift is getting straight As."

Taylor's new educational arrangement allowed her to study anytime, anywhere, which was especially useful as she embarked on a national radio tour. These kinds of tours can be exhausting with long hours, lots of travel, and endless interviews. She was "living in hotel rooms, sleeping in the backs of rental cars as my mom drove to three different cities in one day." But to Taylor, it was a great time. About all those interviews, she wrote, "I loooooved it because it's just talking to people. I could talk to a door." She brought her fiddle player and close pal, Emily Poe, and a guitar player, Todd, with her on the road, playing shows wherever they could.

Sometimes Taylor even went back to school — to play shows. Still self-conscious about her place in the high-school hierarchy, the experience could be nerve-wracking. "I remember when I first started doing high-school shows I was in the 10th grade," she told the *Washington Post*. "So it was a little more intimidating when I was 16 and first got on the road and started doing high-school shows and I'm like, 'Oh, there are seniors out there!'"

But she just immediately started doing so well . . . you just couldn't really think about anything else."

"My brother's always calling me the drop-out of the family," Taylor jokes. "Drop-out" or not, Taylor continued her straight-A streak from her pre-homeschooling days. In fact, Taylor's scholastic success would become something her fans try to emulate. Scott Swift recounted an experience to the *Tennessean* about a man coming up to him and stating

Returning to high school meant remembering the little day-to-day experiences that she'd sacrificed for her career, but Taylor has no regrets about the path she chose. "You're always going to wonder about the road not taken, the dorm not taken, and the sorority not taken," she told CMT. "But if I wasn't doing this, I would've missed out on the best moments I've ever known and the most wonderful life that I still can't believe I get to live."

Taylor Swift

Taylor's self-titled debut album came out on October 24, 2006. It sold 39,000 copies in its first week, giving it the second-highest first-week sales for the year. (Taylor only fell behind friend Kellie Pickler, a defeat she's likely okay with!) It peaked at number one on the Billboard Top Country Albums chart and at number five on the Billboard 200, remaining on the chart for an incredibly long time. In fact, *Taylor Swift* set the record for the longest-charting album since Nielsen SoundScan started tracking sales in 1991, and after 157 weeks *Taylor Swift* passed Nickelback's *All the Right Reasons* to achieve the longest chart reign of the decade. The album went platinum a mere seven months after its release, and Taylor became the first solo female country artist to write or co-write every song on a platinum record.

At the time of its release Taylor's album didn't get as much media attention as her later albums would, but *Taylor Swift* was still well received. *AllMusic* reviewer Jeff Tamarkin noted that Taylor was equipped with "a fresh, still girlish voice, full of hope and naïveté, but it's also a confident and mature one," and added, "That Swift is a talent to be reckoned with is never in doubt." An About.com reviewer noted that Taylor "writes and sings with the passion and conviction of a veteran of country music." Later, the *New York Times* would hail the album as a "small masterpiece of pop-minded country."

Taylor followed up "Tim McGraw" with singles "Teardrops on My Guitar," "Our Song," "Picture to Burn," and "Should've Said No." All of them hit the top 10 on the Country Songs chart, and each song also found a spot on the Hot 100 list. Taylor had achieved the gold standard (or, more accurately, platinum standard) of music industry success — she had crossover appeal. Pop music listeners took to her songs almost as eagerly as country fans did.

Nashville producer and performer John Rich explained, "You can hear great pop sensibilities in her writing as well as great storytelling, which is the trademark of old-school country song-crafting." Since her days belting out Dixie Chicks songs at karaoke contests, Taylor has known that her roots are in country music, and she's glad that her songs are drawing new fans to the genre. "I'd like to think that country music is where I live, country music is who I am, but I'm lucky enough to have other people listening who aren't necessarily core country music fans," said the singer. With her solid presence on the pop charts, Taylor has followed in the footsteps of the women she idolized as a child — LeAnn Rimes, Shania Twain, the Dixie Chicks, and Faith Hill. Despite Taylor's crossover success, Scott Borchetta still makes the country music crowd the label's first priority when it comes to all things Taylor Swift. "They're always going to get the singles first, always going to be first in line at the meet-and-greets," says the CEO. "We overthink everything. One thing we can't do is chase the moving target of pop radio." And Taylor wisely notes, "I'm not about to snub the people who brought me to the party."

Remarkably, she'd also conquered the demographic Nashville bigwigs had told her didn't exist: young, female country music fans. "So many girls come up and say to me, 'I have never listened to country music in my life. I didn't even know my town had a country music station. Then I got your record, and now I'm obsessed,'" relates the singer. "That's the coolest compliment to me." Astounded by the ever-growing Taylor Nation comprised of young women, CMT exec Brian Philips reflected, "From the moment 'Tim McGraw' hit the channel, she began to amass an audience that traditional Nashville didn't know or didn't believe existed, and that is young women, specifically teens. It's as if Taylor has kind of willed herself into being." The path for Taylor's success was also paved by Carrie Underwood's breakthrough in 2005. When then-22-year-old Carrie won season 4 of *American Idol*, the Oklahoma native took her country-pop sound to the top of the charts with her debut album *Some Hearts*, which has since been certified seven-times platinum.

After Taylor's first album experienced similarly staggering success, Scott Borchetta had no difficulty forecasting a bright future for his young star: "My fear is that she'll conquer the world by the time she's 19. She'll get to the mountaintop and say, 'This is it?' Because she's just knocking down all of those goals that we didn't even have for the first album. . . . My job at this point is really to protect her and not burn her out." But with another album and tours already in sight, Taylor wasn't anywhere close to burning out. Instead, Taylor's success was spreading like wildfire.

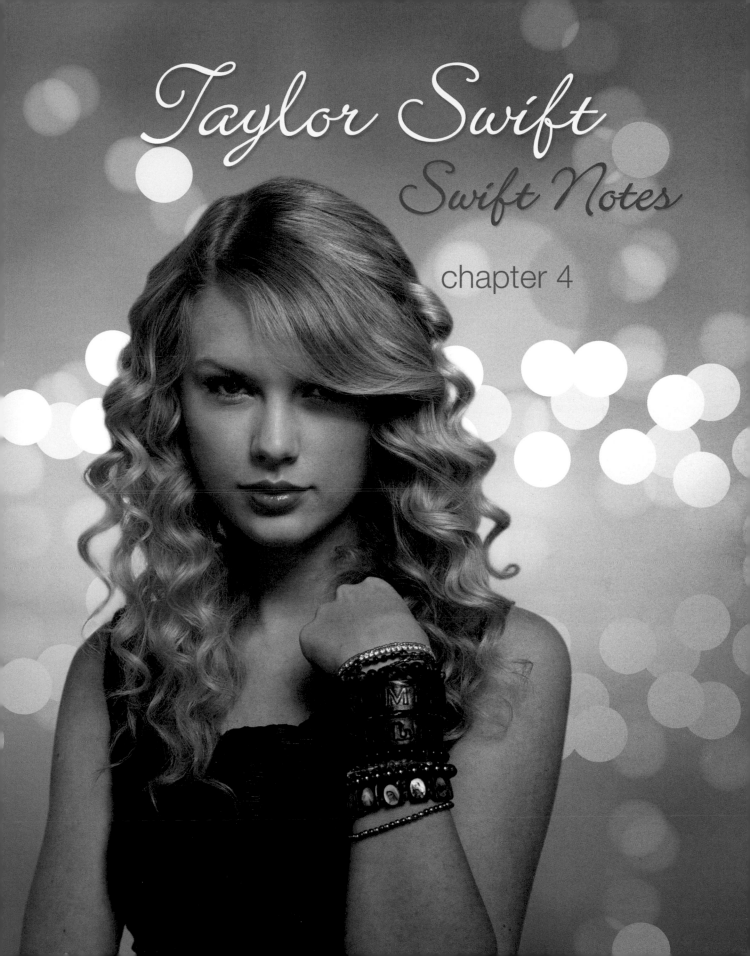

Taylor Swift
Swift Notes

chapter 4

Many of Taylor's songs are about romantic relationships, but her very first and longest love affair is with words, and "Swift Notes" analyzes the songs on her albums just like Taylor dissects her past romances.

BEHIND THE MUSIC: Details on Taylor's inspiration and writing process for the song.

BETWEEN THE LINES: Taylor's an award-winning songwriter; find analysis of her lyrics here.

AUDIENCE OF ONE: Taylor often writes her songs with a very specific audience in mind: "When I sit down and write a song the only person that I'm thinking about in that room is the person that I'm writing the song about and what I want them to know and what I wish I could tell them to their face, but I'm going to say it in a song instead." Wonder if she's singing about someone in particular? Find out in this section.

FUN FACTS: These are extra tidbits about the song and Taylor.

DIARY DECODER: Taylor encodes a secret message into the lyrics in her album booklets; this section solves the puzzles and discusses why Taylor chose that particular message.

YOU SAW IT LIVE: Find details of some of Taylor's special performances of a particular song here.

CHARTING SUCCESS: Taylor's been smashing sales records since her debut. Find out how her singles did and info on awards she's won.

1. "TIM McGRAW"

BEHIND THE MUSIC: Taylor wrote this song during math class in a mere 15 minutes, polished it after school, added piano, and finished it up with Liz!

BETWEEN THE LINES: Despite the fact that his name is mentioned six times, this wistful ballad isn't about the famous country singer, but rather uses Tim McGraw as a sort of musical memento. The song is like a letter to her departed boyfriend, and an actual letter is mentioned in the song's second verse. The Tim McGraw song Taylor sings about is her favorite, "Can't Tell Me Nothin'" from *Live Like You Were Dying*. "Tim McGraw" is about a relationship that ended when the guy left for college ("September was a month of tears" because that's when he went away). The lyrics also reveal what would become part of Taylor's signature style: alternating between a "little black dress" and her more casual "old faded blue jeans."

AUDIENCE OF ONE: Taylor went out with the boy this song's about (rumored to be Brandon Borello) when she was a freshman and he was a senior. Though they may be broken up, he's still a Taylor Swift fan: "He bought the album and said he really loved it, which is sweet," said Taylor. "His current girlfriend isn't too pleased with it, though." And what did Tim McGraw himself have to say about it? "It was awesome, except that I didn't know if I

Taylor introduces herself to Tim McGraw at the ACM Awards on May 15, 2007.

should take it as a compliment or if I should feel old," said the country star. "But the more I hear it . . . I start taking it as a compliment."

FUN FACTS: Since releasing "Tim McGraw," Taylor's become great friends with Tim and his wife, Faith Hill. Tim and Faith even invite Taylor to stay in their home when she visits Los Angeles.

DIARY DECODER: The secret message is "Can't Tell Me Nothin," the Tim McGraw song Taylor had in mind while writing her song.

YOU SAW IT LIVE: At the 2007 ACM Awards, Taylor performed in front of the song's namesake, and finished up "Tim McGraw" standing right in front of Tim McGraw, who was in the front row. She famously extended her hand

and said, "Hi, I'm Taylor," only to be rewarded with a hug from the country music icon.

CHARTING SUCCESS: Taylor's first single peaked at number six on the Billboard Country Songs chart, and number 40 on the Hot 100. "Tim McGraw" was certified gold on May 3, 2007, and later went platinum. Its video won the Breakthrough Video of the Year award at the 2007 CMT Music Awards. Taylor was shocked by its success, saying, "It never really occurred to me that that song would be so relatable."

2. "PICTURE TO BURN"

BEHIND THE MUSIC: One day Taylor arrived at her after-school job at Sony in a rage about a boy. She started playing her guitar and venting, "I hate his stupid truck that he doesn't let me drive. He's such a redneck! Oh my God!" Some of those very words found their way into the song's chorus.

BETWEEN THE LINES: Taylor told the *Washington Post*, "It's about a guy I liked who didn't like me back, and I got really mad, you know?" The two never officially dated because, Taylor explains, "It really bothered me that he was so cocky and that's where that song came from."

AUDIENCE OF ONE: Taylor's not sure if he knows about this song, but if he does, hopefully he's learned a thing or two and now lets his girlfriend drive his pickup truck.

FUN FACTS: When she was younger, one of Taylor's favorite karaoke songs was the Dixie Chicks' "Goodbye Earl," a song with a similar message — don't get mad, get even. You'll hear a slightly different version of this song on the radio — the line "That's fine, I'll tell mine that you're gay" is replaced with "That's fine, you won't mind if I say," since Taylor never meant to offend anyone.

DIARY DECODER: "Date nice boys" — wise advice, indeed.

YOU SAW IT LIVE: Taylor gave a blazing performance at the 2008 CMT Music Awards as well as on *Live with Regis and Kelly* on April 20, 2008.

CHARTING SUCCESS: The fourth single from Taylor's first album, "Picture to Burn" hit number three on the Billboard Country Songs chart and number 28 on the Hot 100. Looks like pop music fans like their country songs with a little fire in them! "Picture to Burn" was also included on the 2008 compilation of country hits *Now That's What I Call Country*. The song was certified gold on June 11, 2008.

3. "TEARDROPS ON MY GUITAR"

BEHIND THE MUSIC: Taylor wasn't actually crying over her guitar when the idea for this sad song came to her; she was on her way home from school.

BETWEEN THE LINES: "Teardrops on My Guitar" is about Taylor's crush on her friend Drew Hardwick, who liked to talk to Taylor about his girlfriend all the time. Taylor explained to *Seventeen*, "I had it bad for him. And I just kept thinking, 'Why am I so invisible to him? Why does he have to have a girlfriend?' I never told him that I liked him, but I did write a song with his name on it." Taylor further explored this feeling of "girl-next-door-itis," as she calls it, in "You Belong with Me." Teardrops on her guitar is a great image of Taylor working through the tough stuff with music.

AUDIENCE OF ONE: Two years after the song came out, Taylor was heading to a hockey game

with Kellie Pickler and Carrie Underwood when she got quite a surprise: "[Drew] was standing there in my driveway. I haven't talked to this guy in two years. I was like, 'Um, hi?' It would have been really cool and poetic if he had turned up at my house right after my album came out. But it was two years later. A couple of things had happened in my life since then. I was like, 'It's really great to see you. But you're a little late.'"

FUN FACTS: The striking cover image of this single made a second appearance on Taylor's 2007 Christmas album, *Songs of the Season*.

DIARY DECODER: This message reads, "He will never know" but, of course, after Drew showed up on her driveway, Taylor knows he does.

YOU SAW IT LIVE: Taylor performed "Teardrops on My Guitar" with 14-year-old *America's Got Talent* finalist Julienne Irwin on August 21, 2007, as well as on *TRL* on February 27, 2008 and on NBC's *Today* on May 29, 2009.

CHARTING SUCCESS: "Teardrops" rose to number two on the Billboard Country Songs chart, and number 13 on the Hot 100. It also hit the top 10 on the Pop Songs, Adult Pop Songs, and Adult Contemporary lists. "Teardrops on My Guitar" won Song of the Year at the 2008 BMI Country Awards for getting the most airtime of any country song that year. The song was certified gold in 2007 and hit double platinum in 2009.

4. "A PLACE IN THIS WORLD"

BEHIND THE MUSIC: Inspiration for this song struck Taylor as she walked the streets of Nashville shortly after moving there. She told GAC, "I was just sort of looking around at all these big buildings and these important people

and wondering how I was going to fit in."

BETWEEN THE LINES: Taylor wrote this song about trying to make it in Nashville, but the song relates to any major life change, big risk, or just trying to figure out where we fit in. As Taylor has shown her fans, pursuing goals despite your trepidation can really pay off!

AUDIENCE OF ONE: A lot of her songs are written for other people, but this one is really written for Taylor, or for the Taylor she wanted to be. Looking back, Taylor said, "I feel like I finally figured it out."

FUN FACTS: "A Place in This World" is also the name of the GAC *Shortcuts* special on Taylor, included on the deluxe edition of *Taylor Swift*.

DIARY DECODER: "I found it" — great reassurance that it's worth taking a leap of faith if you're "ready to fly."

5. "COLD AS YOU"

BEHIND THE MUSIC: "Cold as You" emerged from a songwriting session with Liz, and although Taylor thinks it contains "some of the best lyrics I've ever written in my life," she didn't come up with the hook until halfway through the songwriting process. She told *Rolling Stone*, "I love a line in a song where afterward you're just like *burn*."

BETWEEN THE LINES: In another track about unrequited love, Taylor explores a relationship with someone who doesn't appreciate her. "It's about that moment where you realize someone isn't at all who you thought they were, and that you've been trying to make excuses for someone who doesn't deserve them. And that some people are just never going to love you," explains the songwriter.

AUDIENCE OF ONE: Taylor chose not to single out

the guy with the icy heart, but the folks back in her hometown like to speculate. "You go out into this big world, and you go back and it's still a small town and they still gossip about it. I think it's one of everybody's favorite things to talk about — who my songs are written about," said Taylor. "There are definitely a few more people who think that I've written songs about them than there actually are."

DIARY DECODER: More great advice: "Time to let go." Was the message for Taylor herself?

6. "THE OUTSIDE"

BEHIND THE MUSIC: This is one of the very first songs Taylor wrote, when she was 12 and wasn't fitting in at school.

TAYLOR SWIFT: DELUXE EDITION

On November 6, 2007, fans who were crying out for more Taylor were rewarded with the release of a deluxe edition of *Taylor Swift*. The album contained three previously unreleased songs that Taylor calls "some of my favorites" from her demo-making days at age 14 and 15, plus a recording of Taylor's first phone call with Tim McGraw. The first new song, "I'm Only Me When I'm with You," talks about finding a person who loves you for who you are. It's a philosophy that Taylor embraces 100%. She told *Seventeen*, "The guy I'm looking for is the guy I can be me around, not a version of me I think he'd like." Taylor released a video for this song, which used home movie footage, and tided fans over until the "Picture to Burn" video came out. She noted, "I think it's the only video CMT has probably ever played that cost, like, five dollars to make." The second tune, "Invisible," revisits the themes of "Teardrops on My Guitar." The third new track, "A Perfectly Good Heart," pleads with an unnamed heartbreaker as Taylor tries to figure out how to make her heart whole again. The CD came with a DVD featuring Taylor's previously released videos, behind-the-scenes featurettes, performance footage, her GAC *Shortcuts* series "A Place in This World," and a special home video compiled by the singer herself.

BETWEEN THE LINES: Most people feel like an outsider at some point, and for Taylor that time was in middle school. She confided to *Entertainment Weekly*, "I wrote that about the scariest feeling I've ever felt: going to school, walking down the hall, looking at all those faces, and not knowing who you're gonna talk to that day. People always ask, 'How did you have the courage to walk up to record labels when you were 12 or 13?' It's because I could never feel the kind of rejection in the music industry that I felt in middle school." Being on the outside did have its benefits: it fueled Taylor's songwriting and encouraged her to embrace what made her different. Taylor writes, "I tried to take the road less traveled by," a reference to the famous Robert Frost poem, "The Road Not Taken," in which he writes, "I took the one less traveled by, / And that has made all the difference." Looks like it did for Taylor too.

AUDIENCE OF ONE: This is a song for all the people who made Taylor feel excluded. Did they get the message? Hopefully. One thing's for sure: many of the mean girls who made her feel so alone had a change in attitude when Taylor hit the big time. Taylor told *Teen Vogue*, "I played a hometown show about a year into my career, and they showed up wearing my T-shirts and asking me to sign their CDs. It was bittersweet, because it made me realize that they didn't remember being mean to me and that I needed to forget about it too. And really, if I hadn't come home from school miserable every day, maybe I wouldn't have been so motivated to write songs. I should probably be thanking them!"

(NOT SO) FUN FACTS: A study found that almost 30% of kids and teens in the U.S. are involved in bullying (that's over 5.7 million people!). For more information about bullying and support groups, go to bullying.org.

DIARY DECODER: This secret message reads, "You are not alone." Even though being excluded can make you feel completely alone, people everywhere are going through the same thing. So at the very least, it's some comfort to know that you're never alone in feeling alone.

CHARTING SUCCESS: This song was not a single, but it was Taylor's first-ever release, appearing on *Chicks with Attitude* in 2004.

7. "TIED TOGETHER WITH A SMILE"

BEHIND THE MUSIC: Taylor wrote this song after finding out a friend was bulimic. It was a revelation that the songwriter describes as "one of those moments when your heart kinda stops." And though Taylor had written about painful things before, she notes, "This one was tough to write, because I wasn't just telling some sad story. This was real."

BETWEEN THE LINES: "Tied Together with a Smile" explores the notion that people aren't always what they seem, that the most outwardly confident person could actually be the most vulnerable. The friend who Taylor wrote it about was a pageant queen, "the golden one" she references in the song. "Girls want to be her and guys want to be with her," said Taylor. Though "The Outside" explains how

hard it can be to be excluded from the in-crowd, "Tied Together with a Smile" shows that being popular has its own set of challenges. "This song is basically about the girls I know, and the difficult things I saw them go through," explained Taylor. "I've never seen this song as a lecture. It's really about how no matter what my friends go through, I'm always going to love them."

AUDIENCE OF ONE: This is a sad story with a happy ending — Taylor's friend got help and is healthy once again.

(NOT SO) FUN FACTS: The National Institute for Mental Health found that one in five women struggle with some kind of eating disorder. Luckily there are lots of great organizations that can help. In the U.S., the National Eating Disorders Association is a great source of information and also provides a referral service (www.nationaleatingdisorders.org; 1-800-931-2237). In Canada, the National Eating Disorder Information Centre provides similar services (www.nedic.ca; 1-866-NEDIC-20).

DIARY DECODER: People with eating disorders struggle with self-image and self-worth; "You are loved" is one of the most important messages they can get.

8. "STAY BEAUTIFUL"

BEHIND THE MUSIC: Taylor's songs may make it seem like she's had a lot of boyfriends, but she didn't date all the boys she's singing about. In "Stay Beautiful," the songwriter merely admired her crush from afar. She explains, "This song is about a guy I thought was cute, and never really talked to much. But something about him inspired this song, just watching him."

BETWEEN THE LINES: "Stay Beautiful" is a reminder of how perfect things appear from a distance; you can imagine pictures in your mind rather than have real pictures to burn when things turn sour! With "Stay Beautiful" following "Tied Together with a Smile" it seems like the lyrics "You're beautiful / Every little piece love, don't you know / You're really gonna be someone, ask anyone" are also wonderful reassurance for those, like Taylor's friend, who can't see that for themselves.

AUDIENCE OF ONE: This song's for Cory, and there's no doubt he'd be flattered to hear it!

FUN FACTS: Taylor has another song about admiring someone from afar on *Fearless: Platinum Edition*, but in "SuperStar" that person is untouchable because he's a celeb.

DIARY DECODER: Taylor's not always serious, and the playful message "Shake N Bake" is a bit of a mystery. Maybe she liked Cory as much as this savory dinner staple?

9. "SHOULD'VE SAID NO"

BEHIND THE MUSIC: Taylor penned this raging tune at the studio right after confronting a boyfriend who was cheating on her. She wrote it just in time to squeeze it onto the album at the last minute. She admitted on her blog, "I wrote it about 20 minutes before we recorded it. It just kind of fell out of my mouth and now it is in my CD player."

BETWEEN THE LINES: "Should've Said No" is the second angry anthem on the album, but has a different message than "Picture to Burn." In this case the focus falls more on bad decision-making than on the guy. Taylor explains, "Just being a human being, I've real- ized that before every big problem you create for yourself, before every huge mess you have to clean up, there was a crucial moment where you could've just said no." Straight-as-an-arrow Taylor doesn't just preach it; she lives it and is often in the media spotlight for being a teen performer who *hasn't* gone off the rails. Taylor credits her folks for her good decision-making, saying, "My parents have instilled a great level of trust in me and I think that's a huge, huge part of who I am. I can tell my mom everything, and I do. Before I make decisions, I always think, 'What is my mom going to think if I tell her this? Is my mom going to be really upset if she finds out that I did this?' Usually I decide, 'No, I'm not going to go through with this.'"

AUDIENCE OF ONE: Thanks to the secret message, it's clear this song's for Sam, and though he hasn't commented about the public sham-ing, Taylor wasn't done with him after her first album. Before the release of *Fearless*, Taylor told *Girls' Life*: "I wrote a few more songs on this upcoming record about him just because, you know, I wasn't done being mad about it. I know he's on the edge of his seat waiting."

FUN FACTS: Sam should have followed Taylor's lead — she says "no" eight times in this song.

DIARY DECODER: This message is a pointed fin-ger: "Sam Sam Sam Sam Sam."

YOU SAW IT LIVE: Taylor belted out "Should've Said No" with the Jonas Brothers in *Jonas Brothers: The 3D Concert Experience*. Taylor also performed the song at the 2008 ACM Awards, starting in a hoodie and baggy jeans, which were then ripped off to reveal a short black

dress. And that performance's finale really made a splash — Taylor shocked the audience by getting soaked by an onstage waterfall (an effect that became part of her Fearless Tour).

CHARTING SUCCESS: "Should've Said No" was Taylor's second number one on the Billboard Country Songs chart, and hit number 33 on the Hot 100. The song was certified gold on September 3, 2008, and platinum on October 12, 2009.

10. "MARY'S SONG (OH MY MY MY)"

BEHIND THE MUSIC: Taylor wrote this song after the couple next door came over for dinner and told the Swift family about how they met as children and later fell in love.

BETWEEN THE LINES: After the anger in "Should've Said No," it's nice to follow with a song where a romance worked out. "Mary's Song" follows the couple as they go from being playmates to the beginning of their romance to the proposal and wedding. It's a song brimming with love and hope, and Taylor noted, "I thought it was so sweet, because you can go to the grocery store and read the tabloids, and see who's breaking up and cheating on each other (or just listen to some of my songs, haha). But it was really comforting to know that all I had to do was go home and look next door to see a perfect example of forever."

AUDIENCE OF ONE: This song is for Mary and her husband; maybe one day Taylor will write a new verse about their continued happiness.

FUN FACTS: Taylor and Liz share their co-writing credit on this song with Brian Dean Maher, a Nashville songwriter.

DIARY DECODER: This romantic tune has an appropriately hopeful message: "Sometimes love is forever."

11. "OUR SONG"

BEHIND THE MUSIC: In ninth grade, Taylor realized she and her boyfriend didn't have a song. Inspiration struck while she was sitting in her living room; she "sat down one day with my guitar and got in a groove" and wrote him a song, one that she would perform in front of all of Hendersonville High at the talent show.

BETWEEN THE LINES: Taylor chose to end the album on a high note with this infectious tune about all the ordinary things that can be part of a great love. Right at the end of the chorus, Taylor slyly says, "Play it again" in hopes that listeners would give her record another spin!

AUDIENCE OF ONE: With this final song, Taylor's first high-school romance is the focus of the first and last tracks on the album. And though she is no longer in touch with that boyfriend anymore, he must be just as pleased with the album as when he was in the audience at the talent show.

FUN FACTS: This became Taylor's third single because it was a fan favorite in concert. Don't confuse this song with another popular ballad, Elton John's "Your Song," which is also about writing a song for a loved one.

DIARY DECODER: The album's last secret message, "Live in love," applies not just to "Our Song," but *Taylor Swift* as a whole. The album features everything from first love to fury, and these highs and lows are part of living life to the fullest. And if life and love are just the way Taylor sings it, who would want to miss a moment?

YOU SAW IT LIVE: In one of her earliest award-show performances, Taylor sang "Our Song" at the 2007 CMA Awards. In addition to singing this number on *Regis and Kelly* and on *Ellen*, Taylor rocked out to "Our Song" from the middle of the crowd on *Today* live from Rockefeller Center on May 29, 2009.

CHARTING SUCCESS: "Our Song" was Taylor's first number one, and she refused to give up her spot for six weeks! That six-week stay at the top of the Country Songs chart ties her with one of her heroes, Faith Hill, and her song "Breathe," and both women are topped only by the reign of Connie Smith's 1964 song "Once a Day." "Our Song" also made Taylor the youngest person to write a number-one single on her own. The song also hit number 16 on the Hot 100 and number 24 on the Pop 100, continuing Taylor's crossover success that began with "Teardrops on My Guitar." "Our Song" won Video of the Year at the 2008 CMT Music Awards. The "Our Song" single has earned double platinum certification.

SONGS OF THE SEASON:
THE TAYLOR SWIFT HOLIDAY COLLECTION

A major celebration in the Swift home, Christmas is Taylor's favorite holiday. She wrote on her blog, "I love everything about this time of year, but mostly the way that people find ways to be with the ones they love." With her love of all things Christmas, it was a natural choice for her to release a holiday album. On October 14, 2007, Big Machine released the limited-edition album exclusively in Target and online. Despite these restrictions, the album still climbed to number 14 on the Billboard Top Country Albums chart and to number 20 on the Hot 200.

Taylor covered four Christmas classics: "White Christmas" (originally performed by Bing Crosby), "Santa Baby" (originally performed by Eartha Kitt, and later by Madonna), "Last Christmas" (originally performed by Wham!), and the traditional "Silent Night." Never one to only sing other people's compositions, Taylor added a couple of original songs that offered a twist on the usual seasonal fare. She insisted, "There's got to be something really original and different about it." The heartbreaking "Christmases When You Were Mine" (co-written with Liz Rose and producer Nathan Chapman) is about remembering love from Christmases past, and "Christmas Must Be Something More" encouraged people to see past the gifts to the sacred spirit of the season.

Though the album was supposed to be a one-time release, Taylor Swift fans who still hope to see this album under the tree are in luck; it was re-released in October 2009.

Learning From Legends

In April 2007, Taylor returned to Pennsylvania to play the Sovereign Performing Arts Center in Reading.

"I just went to a show by a future superstar," starts an About.com review of a performance Taylor gave on May 30, 2007, at the Gold Country Casino. With a hot new album on their hands, Big Machine was trying to give Taylor all the exposure she could get, and Taylor played some of her first headlining shows. Her career was picking up speed, and nowhere was that more evident than when she returned to her hometown to play a concert at the Sovereign Performing Arts Center in Reading, Pennsylvania. It was a place where

Taylor had once been in the audience, gazing at performers like Melissa Etheridge from afar. Now, just a few years later, she was center stage, telling the crowd about her journey by paraphrasing one of her favorite songs, Eminem's "Lose Yourself." "See, when I left three years ago," she told the crowd, "I had one shot, one opportunity to seize everything I ever wanted. Y'all think I did alright?"

Though she continued to do some head-lining gigs where she could, Taylor racked up most of her experience touring as an opener

Says Taylor of Kellie Pickler: "She's like a sister. People say we're such opposites, but that's what makes us such good friends. She's incredibly blunt. I love that about her. If some guy has said or done something to me she doesn't like, she'll grab my cell phone and say, 'I'm deleting his number.'" The two co-wrote Kellie's first top 10 hit "Best Days of Your Life," with Taylor singing on the track and appearing in its video.

By 2009, Taylor was not just opening for country legends, she was sharing the stage with them. Pictured here with Rascal Flatts, Carrie Underwood, Brooks & Dunn, and Sugarland at the ACMs on April 5.

for country greats. In October 2006, she hit the road with Rascal Flatts, the three-man country act known for hits such as "What Hurts the Most," "Bless the Broken Road," and a cover of Tom Cochrane's "Life Is a Highway," which was on the soundtrack to Pixar's *Cars*. Finding out she'd be part of her first major tour, Taylor wrote, "I'm SO excited and I can't even express to you how loud I screamed when I found out." She played nine acoustic shows with the group, and Taylor really meshed with the trio, and she toured again with them two years later. During her 2008 tour with the band, she wrote on her blog, "The Rascal Flatts tour is SO much fun. I'm loving it so much, and the guys are so cool. They'll just walk onto my bus and say hi. It's so cool that the guys from Rascal Flatts are so down to earth." Though she dreamed of having a tour to call her own, Taylor wisely realized that she could learn a lot from touring with industry pros. She explained, "I didn't mind opening for Rascal Flatts because you learn something from every single tour you go on, and I felt I had more to learn."

The next stop on Taylor's tour of country star tours was a gig opening for the King of Country himself, George Strait, from January to March 2007. On her blog, Taylor gushed, "I'm pretty much a George Strait superfan, so this is going to be SO much fun." Sure enough, playing with the legendary country icon was thrilling for the young star. Taylor wrote, "I'm pretty sure the highlight of my night last night (the first show of the tour, in Lafayette, LA) was that . . . George Strait SAID MY NAME . . . [We] were watching George's show . . . and all of a sudden he says, 'I'm very happy to have the talented Miss Taylor Swift out here with us.' YESSSSS. It was pretty awesome, sort of a life changing moment."

But her encounters with country music's finest didn't end there — Taylor's next tour would be with country rocker Brad Paisley on his 2007 Bonfires & Amplifiers tour. Brad told *Blender*, "I was looking at a lot of artists to come out on tour with us, but as soon as I downloaded her album, I knew we had to have her. I was floored by the songwriting. I love the fact that she doesn't pretend to be 30 years old in her songs. She has a very genuine voice." Taylor knew she had a lot to learn from Brad, and noted, "I try to pick his brain and learn as much as I can from him."

Also on the Bonfires & Amplifiers tour were labelmate Jack Ingram and pal Kellie Pickler. The three injected a lot of energy and more than a little silliness into the tour like the night they decided to prank the headliner. Taylor ordered tick costumes for her and

If you missed Taylor when she was an opening act, here's an example of her set list from an April 10, 2008, show in Sacramento, CA.

- "I'm Only Me When I'm with You"
- "Our Song"
- "Teardrops on My Guitar"
- "Should've Said No"
- "Tim McGraw"
- "Picture to Burn"

Kellie, and Jack put together an exterminator suit. When Brad started playing his new song "Ticks," Kellie and Taylor emerged in costume, and danced around Brad onstage. Out came Exterminator Ingram who pretended to spray them with insecticide then the bugs faked an elaborate death. Writing about it on her MySpace, Taylor recalls, "I was laughing so hard I could barely breathe. Then I was laying there on the stage playing dead, and looked up at Brad, and he looked down at me and said, 'Nice work.'" Guess he was a little bit "bugged." Not to worry, Brad was a prankster himself, and forced Jack Ingram into a cage and made him perform from there!

While Brad was on a break from touring, Taylor opened shows for another country great, Kenny Chesney. Once again, the person she idolized did not disappoint in real life. "Opening up for Kenny Chesney is one of the coolest things I've ever done," said Taylor. "His tour has this laidback vibe to it, and everyone's so cool to work with. And Kenny Chesney is so completely nice. Genuinely nice."

The rising star learned something from all of her mentors on tour, summing up for *USA Weekend*, "Kenny is up at the crack of dawn, walking around the venue, getting to know everyone from the sound-check guys to the people who sell the souvenirs to the fans. Then Rascal Flatts stages this big production with all the flash. And George Strait? It's all about the music with him. He pays so much attention to building up the song with the arrangements and the band and his singing."

In the summer of 2007, the rising star hit another major career milestone when she toured with two people who inspired her love for country music in the first place — Tim McGraw and Faith Hill. Taylor played a four-song acoustic set before the dynamite duo performed on their Soul2Soul II tour. Getting to know the artists she idolized could have been a real letdown, but Taylor found the couple to be as wonderful as she'd always imagined them. Of Faith she wrote, "As beautiful as she is, she is THAT nice."

Even when Taylor only played a handful of songs as an opening act, reviewers took note. When she opened for Rascal Flatts in early 2008, one reviewer remarked, "If Swift's performance last night was any indication of what the future has to bring, surely there will be many more Grammy nominations, and eventually wins for the young songstress." What an accurate prediction!

Though Taylor confesses, "I've always wanted to be so busy I couldn't stand it," she still managed to get the occasional break from touring, and would head back to Hendersonville. On one such break, she wrote, "I just got back from a five show run on the road. Now I'm sitting in my kitchen . . . on the counter. Eating cool whip. And trying to think of things to do with my free time. Other than talking to my cat and making playlists of sad songs." Though it was nice to be reunited with her entire family, the overachiever didn't like to sit still too long — there were charts to climb, airwaves to conquer, and crowds to entertain. She admitted to *Bliss*, "I do love coming home, but after about a day I usually end up calling my record label and bugging them for something to do."

Golden Girl

As an opener for major country music acts, Taylor spent a lot of her time playing second fiddle to the legendary stars she toured with. But as her first awards season approached in 2007, Taylor was about to prove that she had the chops to be the main event.

With more and more people listening to Taylor's music on MySpace or requesting her songs on the radio, the Taylor Nation of devoted fans was growing every day. And it couldn't have been any clearer than on April 16, 2007, when Taylor took home the fan-voted CMT Music Award in the Breakthrough Video category for "Tim McGraw." Taylor's first award was a sign of the strength of her fans' dedication, which would help raise Taylor to the top of the music industry, and she knew it, offering a thank-you on her blog to all the fans who helped make her dreams come true: "I've always been the girl watching the award shows from the stands or from my couch, wishing like crazy that someday if I worked hard enough and things really came together, that could be me. You did that for me." And as a special thank-you, she brought her award ("The Buckle") with her on the Brad Paisley tour, so fans could see the award they helped her win.

Fans are one thing, but getting industry respect is another. Six months after her CMT Music Award, it became abundantly clear that country music's finest were behind Taylor too. At the 2007 Country Music Association (CMA) Awards on November 7, Taylor won the prestigious Horizon Award, which goes to the most promising new artist of the year. As the previous year's winner Carrie Underwood explained as she presented it, "This is an award that means you have *truly* arrived in country music." Past winners include Garth Brooks, Keith Urban, Brad Paisley, LeAnn Rimes, and the Dixie Chicks. In her acceptance speech, Taylor was sure to thank the fans, tearfully insisting, "You have changed my life!" before finishing, "This is definitely the highlight of my senior year," a comment that got chuckles from the crowd. On her blog, Taylor shared what was going through her mind in this fairytale moment: "I remember it all in slow motion . . . I'm running up the stairs in a ball gown and heels. My mom and dad are crying. Everyone at my record label is screaming. My family and everyone I love is watching from their living rooms. I'm crying on national television, and thinking about [the fans]." She concluded, "And thank you for convincing me that fairytale endings . . . Well, they happen sometimes."

Fearless Songbird

When Taylor sat down in December 2007 to start planning her sophomore album, she knew she had a tough act to follow — her self-titled debut had just been certified double platinum. "Pressure is one of my favorite things in the world," Taylor told the *Tennessean*. "When I heard before my second album, 'Is she going to experience a sophomore slump?' it made me more motivated to make sure that didn't happen. 'Is she going to keep this fan base?' 'Is this thing going to run off the tracks?' Those things motivate me. My gut instinct has worked so far, and I'm not going to mess with that."

One of the positive side effects of her

BEAUTIFUL EYES

The wait between Taylor's first and second albums was a long one for her dedicated fans. So on July 15, 2008, Taylor released *Beautiful Eyes*, six songs packaged with a DVD. The EP, which would only be available online and at Walmart, had two songs which Taylor wrote when she was 13 ("Beautiful Eyes" and "I Heart ?") as well as alternate versions of "Should've Said No," "Teardrops on My Guitar," "Picture to Burn," and "I'm Only Me When I'm with You" (which was on the deluxe edition of *Taylor Swift*). The DVD had all of Taylor's videos, her ACM performance of "Should've Said No," and a special homemade video for "Beautiful Eyes" with footage from her 18th birthday party. "I've gotten so many emails from people asking for new songs, and I thought this might tide them over till the new album comes out in the fall," Taylor explained on her MySpace blog. This limited-run album still managed to top the Billboard Country chart just two weeks after its release, with the number two spot going to Taylor Swift. Overwhelmed by her one-two domination of the charts, the singer blogged, "I can't believe it. My record label is freaking out because apparently the last time this happened was in 1997??" The person who accomplished that in 1997? None other than Taylor's first inspiration, LeAnn Rimes.

tremendous success is that the certified country star had proven she was a girl who knew what she was doing, and she was given even more creative control on her second record. Nathan Chapman, who worked on her first record, was back in the studio to produce, but this time Taylor officially stepped up as co-producer. A lucky 13 tracks would make the cut and appear on *Fearless*, including the last-minute addition "Forever & Always."

Beyond supervising, writing, and recording the music, Taylor was heavily involved in the album design as well. On her MySpace, Taylor wrote, "I'm completely going crazy thinking of ideas for the album photo shoots and the CD booklet and all of that stuff. I'm consumed and obsessed and so excited that I get to make a second record. Hey, I'm still in awe of the fact that I got to make the first one." She and her label found the right photographer, Nashville's Joseph Anthony Baker, and Taylor played the album for him to see which songs spoke to him. What resulted was a gorgeous array of photographs of Taylor inspired by the songs. "We shot photos based on the energy of that song," explained the singer-temporarily-turned-model. And what about the album cover image of Taylor's face framed by a halo of windswept golden curls? "The photographer put the wind machine on, like, hurricane mode," said Taylor. "That's how we got the picture." Taylor oversaw every

aspect of the album down to the smallest details, once again encoding secret messages in her lyrics.

Taylor kept her fans up to date on the album's progress, writing, "This next record is on my mind 24/7, all the time. It never stops. I'm always either listening to a new mix of a song or scanning through pictures to make sure we've chosen the right ones, or wondering which songs you guys are going to like the best. I'm just so obsessed with it right now, all the planning."

The album would be called *Fearless*, a name that Taylor explained in the liner notes: "FEARLESS is not the absence of fear. It's not being completely unafraid. To me, FEARLESS is having fears. FEARLESS is having doubts. Lots of them. To me, FEARLESS is living in spite of those things that scare you to death."

Despite her success, country music's golden girl isn't without her own fears. She explained to *Girls' Life*, "I think things on the record that are talked about have a very fearless quality to them. It's not about me being this fearless person because I'm afraid of everything, you know? I'm afraid of finding the most perfect love and losing it. I'm afraid of regretting things. I'm afraid of my career becoming mediocre and not being able to excite people anymore. I'm afraid of running out of things to write about. But I think there's something fearless about jumping, even when you're really scared of where you might land."

Taylor made that leap on November 11, 2008, with the release of *Fearless*, launching it on *Good Morning America*, just as she had with her first record. In its debut week, *Fearless* hit number one on both the Billboard 200 and the Top Country Albums charts. It would go on to spend eight weeks at number one, making it the first female country album to do so. Her sophomore album sold 217,000 copies on its first day alone, and after only one week in stores it was over halfway to platinum certification, with 592,000 copies sold. One of those copies was Taylor's; she stopped in at the Hendersonville Walmart at midnight to buy one the minute it was released. At that moment Taylor still had butterflies. She admitted, "The night before it came out, I remember staying up all night and thinking, 'Is anyone going to buy it at all?' You always have those last-minute jitters." But the overwhelming support from her fans was the best reassurance Taylor could have ever hoped for. "I've never been more proud of anything in my life . . . I wrote every song on it. I co-produced it. So to have people go out and actually buy it? It's wonderful," she told *Newsday*.

"I think any time you've had this kind of success it starts to get weighty," Scott Borchetta told the *LA Times*. "But she's delivered a brilliant record." For the most part, reviewers agreed. *Rolling Stone* (which honored her with a cover story in March 2009) praised,

"Swift is a songwriting savant with an intuitive gift for verse-chorus-bridge architecture that, in singles like the surging 'Fifteen,' calls to mind Swedish pop gods Dr. Luke and Max Martin. If she ever tires of stardom, she could retire to Sweden and make a fine living churning out hits for Kelly Clarkson and Katy Perry." The reviewer added, "Her music mixes an almost impersonal professionalism — it's so rigorously crafted it sounds like it has been scientifically engineered in a hit factory — with confessions that are squirmingly intimate and true." *Blender* gave it four stars out of five, with the reviewer noting, "Swift has the personality and poise to make these songs hit as hard as gems like 'Tim McGraw' and 'Our Song' from her smash debut, and, once again, she wrote or co-wrote them all." More praise came from *AllMusic*, which concluded, "Swift's gentle touch is as enduring as her song-craft, and this musical maturity may not jibe with her age, but it does help make *Fearless* one of the best mainstream pop albums of 2008."

1. "FEARLESS"

BEHIND THE MUSIC: The idea for this song came to Taylor while she was touring. She didn't have a boyfriend and she started thinking about her ideal first date. She explained, "I think sometimes when you're writing love songs, you don't write them about what you're going through at the moment, you write about what you wish you had. So this song is about the best first date I haven't had yet."

BETWEEN THE LINES: Taylor described "Fearless" as "about an incredible first date when all your walls are coming down and you are fearlessly jumping into love." And what's Taylor's idea of a great first date? She told *Girls' Life*, "I live on a lake, so it's really fun to go out on the boat, and then hang out all night and just talk. It wouldn't have to be anything fancy or anything like that, but just being with a person who gets you. It's kind of funny because you don't ever have a lot of opportunities like that to be home and to go on a date in your hometown, but that's exactly what I would do." Standing in the rain had been associated with the stormy anger of her "Should've Said No" performance at the 2008 ACM Awards, but on the title track of her second album, it's a sign of reckless abandon, of overcoming trepidation for something worthwhile.

AUDIENCE OF ONE: Since this one isn't based on a real-life date, it's not for a specific lucky guy, but the message to be fearless is great advice for everyone.

FUN FACTS: Taylor and Liz share co-writing credits for "Fearless" with Hillary Lindsey, who's penned songs for Bon Jovi, Miley Cyrus, and Martina McBride, but is best known for her work with Carrie Underwood, including the Grammy-winning single "Jesus, Take the Wheel." Colbie Caillat, Taylor's collaborator on "Breathe," also has a song called "Fearless" on her 2009 album, *Breakthrough*. Colbie's is about the end of a relationship and having the courage to carry on after heartbreak.

DIARY DECODER: This optimistic song's message for a future sweetheart says, "I loved you before I met you."

YOU SAW IT LIVE: Taylor debuted "Fearless" in a live performance on the *Late Show with David Letterman* on November 10, 2008, the day before her album's release.

CHARTING SUCCESS: Before "Today Was a Fairytale" landed a higher spot, "Fearless," her fifth single from *Fearless*, was Taylor's highest chart debut on the Billboard Hot 100, sitting at number nine in its first week. "Fearless" also peaked at number 15 on the Country Songs chart. Amazingly, "Fearless" was the first song in Billboard history to be certified gold before it was officially released.

2. "FIFTEEN"

BEHIND THE MUSIC: Taylor started writing this song with the lines, "Abigail gave everything she had / to a boy who changed his mind," which even critics who weren't head over heels for the album singled out as "a great, revealing line about a friend's lost innocence."

BETWEEN THE LINES: Taylor is often praised for speaking authentically about people her age. Fellow country star Vince Gill said, "Every kid relates to Taylor and those songs because they're pointed right at them," and "Fifteen" is a great example of that. It looks back on those vulnerable years at the beginning of high school when you feel like an outsider

Miley and Taylor at the 51st Annual Grammy Awards on February 8, 2009.

and social status can feel like it's everything, when love is the best thing and the worst thing that can happen, when you have no idea where you're headed or who you'll become. "Fifteen" offers great advice for those tumultuous times: this too shall pass. Taylor wisely advised, "Don't make high school everything. Because if high school is everything, then you've got a long life to live, and I'd like to think that the best years of my life are still ahead of me." Taylor further explains, "It says, 'I should have known this, I didn't know that, here's what I learned, here's what I still don't know.'" Taylor skillfully weaves together the two themes of the song — fitting in and falling in love — in one line: "When all you wanted was to be wanted," getting to the heart of a teenager's longing to belong.

AUDIENCE OF ONE: "I think that the song 'Fifteen' is definitely advice to my former self, but it could also be advice to any girl going into ninth grade and feeling like you're the smallest person on the planet," says Taylor.

FUN FACTS: In the summer of 2008, the guy who hurt Abigail came back into her life with a grand gesture: he asked her to come talk to him, and he was waiting in a field, inside a heart made of candles with a big bouquet of roses for her. Taylor even lent a hand to the one-time heartbreaker, telling him all of Abigail's favorite songs so he could put them on a mix CD. But even when life seems as perfectly orchestrated as a romantic movie, love isn't easy, and Taylor admits, "As usual, I had to clean up the mess the next day . . . But that's okay. I didn't mind."

DIARY DECODER: "I cried while recording this" lets listeners know that this is a song that made Taylor shed some teardrops on her guitar.

YOU SAW IT LIVE: Taylor performed "Fifteen" at the 2009 Grammy Awards with real-life pal Miley Cyrus. The pair sat on stools and Taylor played guitar, a pared-down approach to the song that the singer would also use in concert. Asked how then-16-year-old Miley looks back on her 15th year, she replied that, like most teens, she spent that year "thinking you know everything," before realizing "the only thing you're left with are your best friends." "Fifteen" was the second song Taylor performed at the 2009 CMA Awards. Three hundred Hendersonville High students looked on from the audience; Taylor nabbed them free tickets to the show. The singer also played the song on *The View*, *Ellen*, and the U.K.'s *Paul O'Grady Show*.

CHARTING SUCCESS: "Fifteen" peaked at number seven on the Hot Country Songs chart, number 10 on the Pop Songs chart, number 23 on the Hot 100, and also appeared on the Hot Adult Contemporary and the Hot Adult Pop Songs list. Though the song may contain advice for freshmen, adults relate to it too!

3. "LOVE STORY"

BEHIND THE MUSIC: Taylor wrote this song lying on her bedroom floor in a mere 20 minutes and recorded a rough cut of the track in 15 minutes of studio time the next day. She said the song sprang from the line "This love is difficult / but it's real," and she noted on her MySpace, "When I wrote that line, I knew it would be my favorite line to sing every night. And it's true, every time I sing that, I can't help but smile."

BETWEEN THE LINES: "Love Story" follows the plot of *Romeo and Juliet* fairly faithfully. Taylor's Juliet is on a balcony remembering when she met Romeo, which in Shakespeare's play is also at a party. The two lovers meet again in a garden (in the play it's an orchard), and Romeo must leave town, though in the song it's because Juliet's family disapproves, whereas in *R&J* there's a more serious reason — Romeo kills Juliet's cousin, Tybalt. Taylor's love story ends with a happy ending in marriage, and though Romeo and Juliet marry in Shakespeare's tale, it is done hastily and in

secret without either family's approval. Discussing her rewrite of the famous double-suicide finale, Taylor said, "I was really inspired by that story. Except for the ending. I feel like they had such promise and they were so crazy for each other. And if that had just gone a little bit differently, it could have been the best love story ever told. And it is one of the best love stories ever told, but it's a tragedy. I thought, why can't you . . . make it a happy ending and put a key change in the song and turn it into a marriage proposal." There's a second literary reference in "Love Story" in the line "'Cause you were Romeo, I was a scarlet letter." *The Scarlet Letter* is a famous novel by Nathaniel Hawthorne about Hester Prynne, a woman who cheated on her husband and is outcast from her community. Though Taylor's Juliet has been faithful, the connection is that, like Hester, Juliet is in an unpopular relationship that upsets the people around her. In the end, the message of this uplifting love anthem comes down to Taylor's favorite line, which means to her that "sometimes you have to fight for love, but sometimes it's worth fighting for."

AUDIENCE OF ONE: Taylor told *Time* that this one's about a guy she never really dated (she calls these boys "nominees") because her friends and family didn't approve. But no doubt her would-be Romeo approves of the happy ending Taylor made up for them.

FUN FACTS: "Love Story" has already been covered by many artists including Intohimo, The Scene Aesthetic, Forever the Sickest Kids, Davedays, Tiffany Giardina, and Savannah Outen and Josh Golden. Fittingly, "Love Story" plays in the trailer for the 2010 film *Letters to Juliet*.

DIARY DECODER: The secret message here is "Some day I'll find this." Even though Taylor's happy being single and despite having had her share of heartbreak, she still believes in love. She told *Seventeen*, "I have to believe in fairytales, and I have to believe in love — but not blindly. If you do meet your Prince Charming, know he is going to have his good days and his bad days. He is going to have days when his hair looks horrible, and days when he's moody and says something that hurts your feelings. You have to base your fairytale not upon happily ever after, but on happy right now."

YOU SAW IT LIVE: Taylor performed the song at Children in Need, a charity show in the U.K., and afterward donated £13,000 to the cause. She also performed it amid screaming fans on *Today*, and on *Dancing with the Stars*, *Ellen*, and at the 2008 CMA Awards.

CHARTING SUCCESS: Listeners across the globe officially fell in love with "Love Story." The song charted in Australia, Austria, Belgium, Canada, Denmark, France, Germany, Greece, Ireland, Japan, Mexico, the Netherlands, New Zealand, Norway, the Philippines, Spain, Sweden, Switzerland, and the United Kingdom. In the U.S., the single topped the Hot Country Songs, Top 40 Mainstream, and Hot Adult Contemporary Tracks charts, as well as hit number three on the Adult Pop Songs chart and number four on the Hot 100. With over four million downloads, "Love Story" is the most downloaded country song in history, and ties Lady Gaga's "Just Dance" for the highest number of downloads for a song by a female artist. In 2008, it won Billboard's Hot Radio Songs of the Year award, and in 2009, it won Country Song of the Year at the BMI Awards, Music Video of the Year at the CMA Awards, and Video of the Year and Female Video of the Year at the CMT Music Awards.

4. "HEY STEPHEN"

BEHIND THE MUSIC: Taylor penned this playful love song for her crush, Stephen Barker Liles, guitar player and vocalist for Love and Theft. The band opened for Taylor as part of her '08 tour, so it's likely this one was written on the road.

BETWEEN THE LINES: This song is like a secret love letter, right from the opening greeting of "Hey Stephen." Some of Taylor's cherished romantic images return, including kissing in the rain and showing up at someone's bedroom window. If all these songs were based on real moments, Taylor's bedroom window would get as much traffic as Dawson Leery's; this romantic gesture also appears in "Our Song," "Love Story," and "Come In with the Rain." And though Taylor insists she never wants to write songs only about being on the road, there's just a hint of it here. The line "Hey Stephen, why are people always leaving? / I think you and I should stay the same" suggests that a life on the road sometimes means too many goodbyes.

AUDIENCE OF ONE: When *Fearless* came out, Taylor texted Stephen saying, "Hey, track 5!" and was rewarded with an email reply from her overwhelmed crush. Stephen told *People*, "We've become great friends since Love and Theft started opening shows for her. I think everyone would agree she's a total sweetheart and anyone would be lucky to go out with her."

For a snippet of Taylor with Stephen, watch her October 19, 2008, MySpace video to see them lip-synch to Katy Perry's "Hot N Cold."

FUN FACTS: The finger snaps on this track are provided by Martina McBride's children and their friends, who were dying to meet Taylor, and jumped at the opportunity during a recording session at John McBride's Blackbird Studio.

DIARY DECODER: "Love and Theft" reveals who the mystery Stephen is. The band was signed to a record deal with Lyric Street Records in 2009, and has released two singles. Perhaps when their full-length album appears, Taylor will get a reply to her love letter.

5. "WHITE HORSE"

BEHIND THE MUSIC: According to *Country Weekly*, this song was written with the guy from "Love Story" in mind. After Taylor composed the first verse, she called Liz Rose, and in about 45 minutes the pair polished off the song that would go on to win a Grammy.

BETWEEN THE LINES: For pessimists, "White Horse" could be "Love Story: Part 2." It's a song about the end of a relationship with no hope for recovery. Taylor explained to *Billboard*, "It's one of the songs that I am really proud of on the record because it's so sparse — guitar, piano, and cello . . . it talks about falling in love and the fairytales that you are going to have with this person, and then there is that moment where you realize that it is not going to happen. That moment is the most earth-shattering moment." Of course, "I'm not a princess / This ain't a fairytale" doesn't mean that true love doesn't exist, just not between these two. Interestingly,

Taylor mentions the "face of an angel" in this song, which is also part of the chorus in "Hey Stephen." Hopefully Stephen wasn't the one to let her down!

FUN FACTS: Originally "White Horse" was going to be saved for Taylor's third album because *Fearless* already had its fair share of sad songs. That decision changed when *Grey's Anatomy* wanted the song for the premiere episode of season 5, "Dream a Little Dream of Me." And while "White Horse" may be about disappointment, for Taylor having a song on her favorite show was a dream come true: "You should've seen the tears streaming down my face when I got the phone call that they were going to use that song. I have never been that excited. This is my life's goal, to have a song on *Grey's Anatomy*. My love of *Grey's Anatomy* has never wavered. It's my longest relationship to date."

DIARY DECODER: "All I ever wanted was the truth" hints that Taylor's prince was a liar and that their fairytale castle wasn't built on solid ground.

YOU SAW IT LIVE: Taylor offered an intimate performance of "White Horse" at the 2008 American Music Awards where she was named Favorite Female Country Artist.

CHARTING SUCCESS: This song earned Taylor two Grammy Awards — one for Best Country Song and one for Best Female Country Vocal Performance. This second single from *Fearless* peaked at number two on the Billboard Hot Country Songs chart, number 13 on the Hot 100, and number 23 on the Pop 100, and also charted in Canada, the United Kingdom, and Australia. The "White Horse" single received platinum certification.

6. "YOU BELONG WITH ME"

BEHIND THE MUSIC: Taylor's inspiration for this song came from eavesdropping while hanging out on her band's bus. Taylor told *Self*, "The guy was going, 'Baby, of course I love you more than music, I'm so sorry. I had to go to sound check. I'm so sorry I didn't stay on the phone.' So immediately in my head, I get this line, 'You're on the phone with your girlfriend she's upset. She's going off about something that you said.' And it all came to me at once. I bolted to my bus [to write it down]." Taylor took the idea to a songwriting session with Liz where the two fleshed out the story, and Taylor notes that "She wears short skirts, I wear T-shirts" was their favorite line to write.

BETWEEN THE LINES: Taylor says she never had a crush on her band member; she just inserted herself into the situation and ran with it. But she does know what it's like to be the invisible girl, as she explored in "Teardrops on My Guitar." She explained, "Basically like 'girl-next-door-itis.' You like this guy who you have for your whole life, and you know him better than she does but somehow the popular girl gets the guy every time."

DIARY DECODER: "Love is blind so you couldn't see me" is a clever reinforcement of the idea that it's often hard to see the good thing right in front of you.

YOU SAW IT LIVE: Taylor Swift performed "You Belong with Me" at the 2010 Grammy Awards accompanied by singer-songwriter and banjo whiz Butch Walker. Butch got the gig in an unconventional way. He posted a cover version of the song online and it caught Taylor's notice (she tweeted, "I'm losing my MIND listening to it! Blown away. This weekend rules").

She called him up and invited him to join her onstage at the Grammys. Butch agreed and played the banjolin (a combination of a banjo and mandolin), just like he did in his cover. He joined her again for the Fearless Tour's stop at L.A.'s Staples Center. Taylor also performed this tune live at the 2009 MTV Video Music Awards, at the 2009 CMT Music Awards, on *Today*, and on *The Jay Leno Show*.

CHARTING SUCCESS: The third single from *Fearless*, "You Belong with Me," was nominated for Song of the Year, Record of the Year, and Best Female Pop Vocal Performance at the 2010 Grammys, although it didn't win. It had better success at the 2009 MTV Video Music Awards where it won Best Female Video. "You Belong with Me" became Taylor's fourth number one hit in the U.S., topping the Hot Country Songs chart and the Hot Adult Contemporary Tracks chart, and scored a number three on the Canadian Hot 100. It also sat at number two on the Pop Songs chart and on the Hot 100, and charted in top 100s all over the world, including in Ireland, New Zealand, and the U.K. "You Belong with Me" has been certified double platinum.

7. "BREATHE"

BEHIND THE MUSIC: Taylor admired Colbie Caillat's first album, *Coco*, so much she was determined to work with her fellow up-and-coming artist. She approached Colbie's management, and Colbie ended up with a day off after a radio-station promotional show in Nashville. After working on some pieces Taylor had written, the two wrote "Breathe" together and Colbie contributed vocals,

recorded at Starstruck Studios. Taylor gushed to MTV, "I just think she's the coolest thing out there right now. So for her to be on my next album makes me feel cooler." Colbie has nothing but praise for Taylor: "She is so sweet, so beautiful, so talented, and honestly just a really intelligent young women. She knows what she is doing and she knows how to handle her career and take charge. I love her."

BETWEEN THE LINES: Before "Breathe," all of Taylor's songs about breakups fell into two categories: laced with anger (like "Picture to Burn" and "Should've Said No") or sad laments about being let down (as in "White Horse" and "Forever & Always"). This downtempo duet explores an ending with no rage and no one to blame; it's about the end of a friendship. She explains, "It's a song about having to say goodbye to somebody, but it never blames anybody. Sometimes that's the most difficult part. When it's nobody's fault."

AUDIENCE OF ONE: Taylor hasn't said which former friend this heart-wrenching tune is for, but on first listen, he or she must have found it a little hard to breathe.

FUN FACTS: "Breathe" shares a title with a famous song by one of Taylor's favorite performers — Faith Hill. Faith's 1999 single was a huge country and pop hit, landing number ones on three different charts. While Colbie didn't win a Grammy for this collaboration with Taylor, she had one in her pocket thanks to her 2009 duet with Jason Mraz on "Lucky."

DIARY DECODER: "I'm sorry I'm sorry I'm sorry" is both the secret message and the soft closing vocals that Taylor added while recording, saying to Colbie, "You never said it in the song, but

Colbie Caillat and Taylor at the BMI's 57th Annual Pop Awards on May 19, 2009.

that's totally what the song's about." The apology is not about taking the blame but rather a wish that things turned out differently.

CHARTING SUCCESS: "Breathe" was nominated for Best Pop Collaboration with Vocals at the 2010 Grammy Awards.

8. "TELL ME WHY"

BEHIND THE MUSIC: Sick of getting mixed signals from a guy, Taylor arrived at a writing session with Liz all riled up and vented to her co-writer. Liz asked, "If you could say everything you were thinking to him right now, what would you start with?" Taylor told her, "I would say to him, 'I'm sick and tired of your attitude, I feel like I don't even know you.'" She remembers, "I just started rambling, and she was writing down everything that I was saying, and so we turned it into a song."

BETWEEN THE LINES: "Tell Me Why" is about a romance gone wrong where the person isn't who she wants him to be and is the kind of guy who makes others feel small to feel better about himself, only acting sweet to stop his girlfriend from leaving. Despite all the song's hurt and disappointment, it ends on a positive note as she walks away from a poisonous relationship.

AUDIENCE OF ONE: Taylor hasn't outed her hot 'n' cold honey, but one thing's for sure, with this song, he wasn't getting any mixed signals from Taylor!

FUN FACTS: "Tell Me Why" shares its title with a 1964 Beatles song that has a similar theme of someone stuck in a miserable relationship: "Did you have to treat me oh so bad / All I do is hang my head and moan."

DIARY DECODER: "Guess I was fooled by your smile" reminds Taylor's fans that appearances can be misleading.

9. "YOU'RE NOT SORRY"

BETWEEN THE LINES: Much like "White Horse," "You're Not Sorry" is about a would-be Prince Charming who's fallen from his pedestal. "It is about this guy who turned out to not be who I thought I was. He came across as Prince Charming. Well, it turned out Prince Charming had a lot of secrets that he didn't tell me about. And one by one, I would figure them out. I would find out who he really was." The discoveries were unpleasant, and Taylor notes, he "kept apologizing and kept doing the same thing over and over again. And after a while I think you just have to stand up to that person and say, 'You're not sorry, at all.'" As the saying goes, "Fool me once, shame on you. Fool me twice, shame on me."

AUDIENCE OF ONE: Taylor hasn't shared the identity of this guy, but if she did, he might finally be sorry!

FUN FACTS: Taylor *and* her music appeared on *CSI* in the episode "Turn, Turn, Turn," which features a remixed version of "You're Not Sorry."

DIARY DECODER: "She can have you" hints that her boyfriend's greatest secret was another woman.

YOU SAW IT LIVE: Taylor made one of the most memorable entrances of her career for her performance of "You're Not Sorry" at the 2009 ACM Awards when David Copperfield made her appear in a seemingly empty cage suspended in the air. Talk about being fooled!

CHARTING SUCCESS: Released as a digital single, "You're Not Sorry" climbed to number

FEARLESS: PLATINUM EDITION

Less than one year after *Fearless* was released, the millions of fans all over the world who had bought that album wanted more. Following the precedent of her first album, Taylor released the platinum edition of *Fearless* on October 26, 2009. It had six new tracks as well as Taylor's videos, behind-the-scenes featurettes on the making of her videos and the Fearless Tour, her CMT Awards "Thug Story" video, and concert photos taken by her brother, Austin. The album's first new track, "Jump Then Fall," is a sweet summer love story, which Taylor calls "really bouncy and happy and lovey." She debuted the song on *Dancing with the Stars* on October 27, 2009, and it was number one on iTunes the week it was released and climbed to number 10 on the Billboard Hot 100. The next track, "Untouchable," is a dreamy number about having a serious crush on someone you can never be with. And though this song sounds like a Taylor Swift original, it's actually written by Nathan and Cary Barlowe of the rock band Luna Halo. Scott Borchetta suggested the song to Taylor when she needed a cover for her appearance on *Stripped*, and she and songwriter Tommy Lee James adapted it. The performance was so popular on YouTube that Big Machine included it on the *Platinum Edition*. In case Joe Jonas didn't get the message the first time, "Forever & Always" was back in a piano version that shows that when the anger's over, sometimes sadness remains. In "Come In with the Rain," Taylor hopes, even if she shouldn't, that a lost love will return, and "SuperStar" is a musical daydream about a famous guy, causing fans to debate whether Joe Jonas had inspired another track in Taylor's song catalog. The last addition to the platinum edition was "The Other Side of the Door," which picks up after a bad fight and vents the frustration of a person too proud to admit she's wrong. Taylor says the song is "all about the dramatics of a relationship." The new songs continued the theme of being fearless, exploring love, and, most importantly, demonstrated Taylor's love for her fans that will last forever and always.

11 on the Billboard Hot 100 within a week of its release. Proof that Taylor can spin her heartache into gold: the RIAA gave this song its gold record in 2009.

10. "THE WAY I LOVED YOU"

BEHIND THE MUSIC: Taylor came up with the concept of a song about dating the good guy while still crushing on the bad guy, and then approached legendary songwriter and musician John Rich with it. "He was able to relate to it because he is that complicated, frustrating messy guy in his relationships. We came at the song from different angles. It was just so cool to get in a room and write with him because he really is an incredible writer," explained Taylor.

BETWEEN THE LINES: "The Way I Loved You" explores the strange logic of love where what's bad for you can seem so good. "It's about being in a relationship with a nice, punctual, practical, logical guy and missing the crazy, complicated, frustrating guy," notes Taylor. Notice the different texture of instrumentation — string instruments and softly plucked banjo for the good guy versus electric guitar and a more rock 'n' roll drumbeat for the bad boy. By the end, the bad boy's sound takes control of the song and maybe Taylor's heart. Taylor takes some of the blame for things going wrong, singing "I'm so in love that I acted insane." The bittersweet message is "breaking down and coming undone" is just part of the wild ride of love.

AUDIENCE OF ONE: If the ex in this song hadn't already been thinking about those tumultuous times, hearing "The Way I Loved You" would likely make them hard to forget.

FUN FACTS: Co-writer John Rich, a Nashville musician, songwriter, and producer, played with the band Lonestar for eight years before embarking on a solo career, then becoming one half of the country duo Big & Rich. John's a prolific songwriter and has published over 100 songs, writing for artists such as Martina McBride, Faith Hill, and Bon Jovi. On working with a co-writer 15 years his junior, he says, "Sure there's an age difference, but she knows herself and her audience very well, and she's so connected to who that audience is. She knows she's still a kid and embraces it. She writes things that are important to her. If she breaks up with a boyfriend, that's traumatic to her, and she'll write about it. Just like if I'm pissed off at the news, I'll write

'Shuttin' Detroit Down.' But we respect that about each other."

DIARY DECODER: "We can't go back" suggests that while she can't forget "screaming and fighting and kissing in the rain," those roller-coaster highs and lows are a thing of the past.

11. "FOREVER & ALWAYS"

BEHIND THE MUSIC: Taylor wrote this song at the *very* end of the recording process, and she had to plead with Scott Borchetta to include it on her album the day before the final version of *Fearless* was submitted.

BETWEEN THE LINES: Taylor writes about the confusion and hurt that comes when someone who seemed committed suddenly gets cold and distant. The songwriter explained, "I'd never had that happen to me before that way, with that abruptness. I thought to myself, 'This needs to be said.' It's a song about watching somebody completely fade away in a relationship and wondering what you did wrong and wondering why things have changed." Taylor's feelings are evident in the changing tempo of the song; she told the *LA Times,* "That emotion of rejection, for me, usually starts out sad and then gets mad. This song starts with this pretty melody that's easy to sing along with, then in the end . . . I'm basically screaming it because I'm so mad. I'm really proud of that." As in most Taylor Swift songs, rain has a role to play, this time its more miserable side represents the heartache of being left in the lurch.

AUDIENCE OF ONE: This one's for Taylor's most high-profile boyfriend, Joe Jonas, with whom she had a very secret relationship and a very public break-up. Asked about the song, Joe

Jonas told *Seventeen*, "It's flattering. It's always nice to hear their side of the story." He was less kind in his musical response; the opening verse to the Jonas Brothers' song "Much Better," goes "I get a rep for breakin' hearts / Now I'm done with superstars / And all the tears on her guitar." Ouch.

FUN FACTS: The platinum edition of *Fearless* also includes a plaintive piano and cello version of "Forever & Always."

DIARY DECODER: "If you play these games we're both going to lose" is the secret message for Joe. With the release of *Fearless: Platinum Edition*, Taylor still didn't have Joe out of her system — the piano version has a different message: "I still miss who I thought he was."

YOU SAW IT LIVE: Taylor's 2009 CMA Awards performance starts with an interview where she admits, "If guys don't want me to write bad songs about them, then they shouldn't do bad things," then the cameras cut to Taylor belting out "Forever & Always" sitting on one of the red chairs that would become familiar set pieces on her Fearless Tour. The opening conversation would appear as well, but with footage featuring *Dateline*'s Hoda Kotb.

12. "THE BEST DAY"

BEHIND THE MUSIC: Taylor wrote this song on the road in the summer and recorded it secretly so she could surprise her mom with it for Christmas.

BETWEEN THE LINES: Though Taylor writes a lot of love songs for the guys in her life, this one is for her family, who not only support her in her career but gave her a wonderful childhood. Taylor mined her childhood memories for the first verse, using a child-like voice to capture the essence of those years. The despair of the second verse contrasts with the happiness of the first, but Taylor's mom pulls her through. Her father also gets some love in the song and there's a shout-out to brother Austin, who may not be famous, but Taylor insists "inside and out he's better than I am." While many of Taylor's songs are filled with anger, loneliness, and pain, "The Best Day" shows us where she got her normally sun-shiny attitude.

AUDIENCE OF ONE: As if the song wasn't special enough, Taylor put her video editing skills to work and pieced together home videos to the track for her mother as a Christmas present. All the work was worth it for her mom's reaction. Andrea told *Dateline*, "The first time that she played 'The Best Day' for me was Christmas Eve. She had made this edited music video. I'm looking on the TV and this video comes up with this voice that sounds exactly like Taylor's. And I looked over at her and she said, 'I wrote it for you, Mom.' And that's when I lost it. And I've lost it pretty much every time I've heard that song since."

FUN FACTS: In May 2009, the video that Taylor created for her mom was made available to fans as part of a special Mother's Day promotion. Fans could go to a Big Machine website and watch the video and send one of three custom e-cards to their mothers.

DIARY DECODER: If Taylor's love for her mom wasn't clear enough in the song, the secret message drives it home with "God bless Andrea Swift."

13. "CHANGE"

BEHIND THE MUSIC: This song started from

Taylor with her mother, Andrea, and brother, Austin.

Taylor's frustration that being on an independent label meant she'd have to work twice as hard to get media attention, to get on a tour, and get nominated for awards. "There were times I was working so hard that I didn't realize that every single day our numbers were getting bigger," Taylor recalled. "Every single day, our fan base was growing. Every single day, the work that we were doing was paying off." But since she couldn't see it yet, Taylor set the song aside until she had a sign that things had changed. That happened on the night she won the Horizon Award. Taylor remembers, "When they called out my name as the Horizon Award winner, I looked over and saw the president of my record label crying. Walking up those stairs, it just occurred to me that that was the night things changed. It changed everything." She completed the song the next night, writing lines that acknowledged her new perspective: "It was the night things changed, / do you see it now?"

BETWEEN THE LINES: The final song on *Fearless* is about challenging expectations and making the impossible possible. For Taylor, it was proving to those non-believing record execs, her teasing classmates, and the industry as a whole that she could not only make it, but rise to the top. Scott Borchetta watched that change happen and notes that this song marks a similar change in her music: "It's one of the few non-love songs that she's recorded so far. Live, it's becoming this tour de force. It's almost like a U2 moment now. So the matu-

ration process is amazing, because she's found a different place where the songs are getting even more important. But it's still her."

AUDIENCE OF ONE: This song is for underdogs everywhere. "When I play it I think about anybody who is on the bottom and knows that someday they want to be somewhere else," says Taylor.

FUN FACTS: "Change" was featured on the AT&T Team USA Soundtrack and played during the highlights montage that closed TV coverage of the 2008 Olympic Games.

DIARY DECODER: While "The Best Day" offers a thank you to the Swift family, this hidden message is for Scott Borchetta: "You made things change for me."

CHARTING SUCCESS: In the true spirit of the song, "Change" overcame some tough competition on the charts, climbing to number 10 on the Hot 100 list.

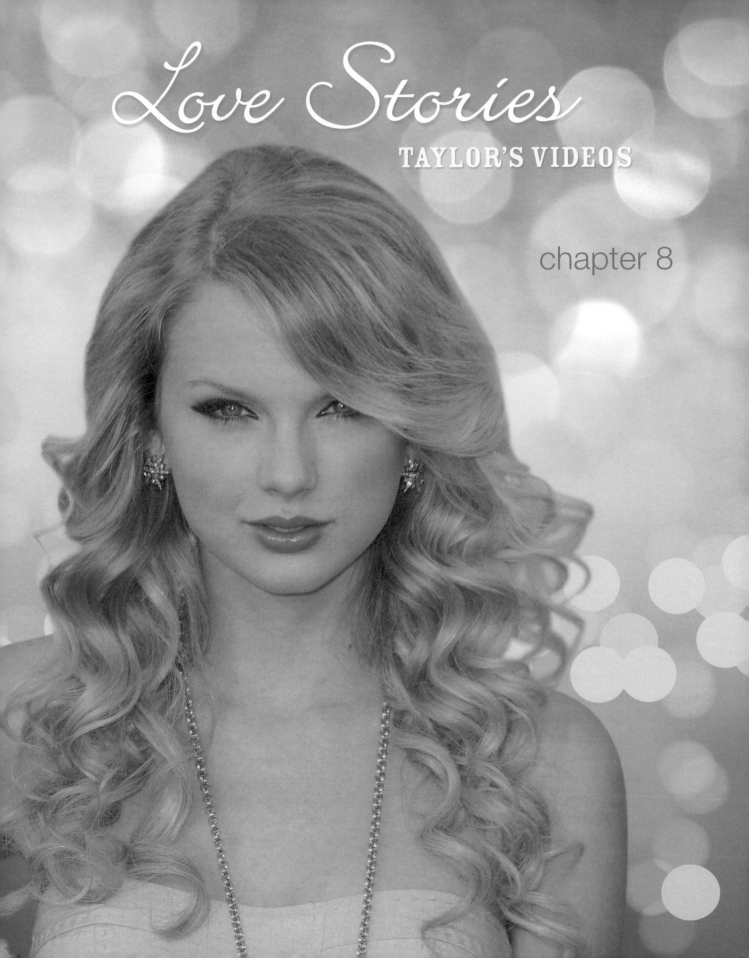

Love Stories

TAYLOR'S VIDEOS

chapter 8

"TIM McGRAW"

THE CONCEPT: Taylor's first music video follows the song's lyrics very faithfully. In a scene that's almost too beautiful to be real, Taylor lays beside a lake as evening approaches. She's holding a radio and singing to her departed boyfriend. While the boyfriend is driving away, he hears a song on his truck's radio that makes him turn back. Between those scenes are flashes of the memories that the Tim McGraw song brings back — horsing around in a field, lying in a pickup truck and looking at the stars, and, of course, slow dancing all night long.

GUEST STARRING: Clayton Collins was chosen because he looked like the guy Taylor wrote the song for.

FUN FACTS: "Tim McGraw" was directed by Trey Fanjoy, who went on to direct five more of Taylor's videos. Trey has also made award-nominated videos with Reba McEntire, George Strait, and Miranda Lambert, but, to date, her only wins come from Taylor Swift videos.

DID YOU NOTICE?: The truck in the video is a Chevy (but it doesn't get stuck as it does in the lyrics). The bracelet Taylor's wearing in the bed of the truck reads "Live In Love." The letter wedged in the cabin door is for "Johnny"; that name was used because that cabin once belonged to country music legend Johnny Cash. While the outside of it looks rustic, the inside has been (appropriately) transformed into a recording studio.

"TEARDROPS ON MY GUITAR"

THE CONCEPT: Fans are familiar with the story behind this song, and the video lays it out well. Taylor's got a crush on Drew, who's unfortunately smitten with another girl. The video alternates between the great times the pair spends together at school and Taylor alone on her bed with only her guitar and those memories for company. Taylor returned to high school, Hume-Fogg High in downtown Nashville, to film this video, an experience she called "a little strange, but in a good way."

GUEST STARRING: Tyler Hilton, a talented actor and musician, plays Drew. He's best known as Chris Keller on the CW's *One Tree Hill* and for playing young Elvis Presley in *Walk the Line*. Taylor happened to read a magazine article where Tyler mentioned being a fan of her music. She invited him to a show, and then offered him the role in the "Teardrops" music video. "He's such a great actor and he brought out a lot in me. You know, because I'm not an actor," said Taylor. "He was really, really cool and it was good to have the chance to become friends with him. He's a sweetheart." Since they didn't want a high school with empty halls, Taylor got to cast some of her friends as extras! Abigail, Kathryn, Kelsey, Ally, Emily, Megan, bro Austin, and her cousin all make an appearance.

FUN FACTS: The aquamarine gown Taylor wears was custom made by stylist Sandi Spika Borchetta, wife of Scott Borchetta, and the dress measures 21 feet long. Taylor managed to wear it on the red carpet of the 2007 CMT Music Awards!

DID YOU NOTICE?: On the fireplace mantle is the Latin phrase *litera scripta manet*. It means "the written word endures," which is one of the reasons Taylor writes songs — to capture her experiences so she won't ever forget them.

In her gown from the "Teardrops" video, Taylor poses with her CMT Music Award on April 16, 2007.

"OUR SONG"

THE CONCEPT: Unlike most of Taylor's videos, "Our Song" doesn't tell a story, instead it lets vibrant colors and symbols of romance do the talking. Trey Fanjoy, who'd directed Taylor's first two videos, dreamed up the concept. The video star related, "When [Trey] heard the song, she had this idea for a front porch performance and then a field of flowers for another performance, then a black-and-white performance shot. It all came together in her head. She was able to translate that so well

Video director Trey Fanjoy, Taylor, stylist Sandy Spika Borchetta, and Big Machine Records' Scott Borchetta embrace backstage at the 2008 CMT Awards.

onto film. It just shows what a truly great director she is."

GUEST STARRING: The only guest stars in this video are Taylor's band, who make their first video appearance.

FUN FACTS: This is the first video that features "Sparkles," Taylor's trademark guitar. Taylor had two dresses custom made for this shoot.

DID YOU NOTICE?: Taylor has a heart on her foot just like in the album booklet (though on the other foot). Even though she said she'd get it permanently tattooed if her first album went double platinum, her dad changed her mind, jokingly threatening he'd take it off with a belt sander! Also, while Taylor's getting ready at the beginning of the video her hair is straight but when she emerges from the house she's got her trademark curls.

"PICTURE TO BURN"

THE CONCEPT: The "Picture to Burn" video starts with Abigail and Taylor parked outside Taylor's ex-boyfriend's place spying on him. Seeing him with another girl (driving his pickup truck!), Taylor has an elaborate revenge fantasy. Taylor joked to CMT, "The storyline of the video is if you break up with me, my band will ransack your house."

GUEST STARRING: The video's bad boy is played by former Tennessee Titans football player Justin Sandy who was a little apprehensive about his villainous role. "I'm gonna have every girl in the United States hate me after this video," he joked. Justin was selected because, according to Taylor, "We wanted him to be classically, like, almost too cute." Abigail Anderson plays a true-to-life role — Taylor's BFF. This was her second time in one of Taylor's videos, but only the back of her head was visible in "Teardrops on My Guitar." Taylor's band members are back, this time with juicy roles as her agents of revenge. "They have the most hilarious sense of humor and I really wanted to portray that in this video," said Taylor. Describing the shoot, Taylor wrote, "My band was in the video a lot, and they were wearing these amazing black business suits and aviators. They looked like secret agents. Except with more highlights." After that shoot, they started referring to themselves as "The Agency."

FUN FACTS: Day one of this video, also known as "pyro day," was shot in the same arena where they film the CMA Awards. Before filming the fire-heavy scenes, Taylor was a little bit nervous about her first pyrotechnic experience, confessing, "There are some things I'm nervous about. My hair could very well catch on fire."

DID YOU NOTICE?: The video uses the radio edit of the song, not the album version.

"LOVE STORY"

THE CONCEPT: Taylor spies her Romeo while walking out of school, and it seems like the two knew each other in another lifetime. Scenes of an elaborate *Romeo and Juliet* fantasy alternate between Taylor waiting for her Romeo in a castle and the couple's story — meeting at a party, sneaking out to meet at night in a garden, and finally, coming together in the field (a scene that Taylor always dreamed of shooting).

GUEST STARRING: Taylor searched for six months to find the right person, before picking Justin Gaston because he "looked very timeless." The model (and one-time close friend of Miley Cyrus) reprised his role as Romeo at the 2008 CMAs when Taylor performed "Love Story." A singer himself, Justin competed on season 6 of the reality show *Nashville Star*, and also appears in the *Glee* pilot.

FUN FACTS: Though the 20 dancers in the party scene are professionals, Taylor had to learn the ballroom dance in 15 minutes! Taylor's two gowns were specially designed for her over a two month period by stylist Sandi Spika Borchetta, who had Taylor's input every step of the way. The video was shot during a heat wave, which felt even hotter for Taylor with tights, a corset, and a heavy

Justin Gaston joins Taylor onstage as she performs "Love Story" at the 2008 CMAs.

dress on. The corset was a bigger challenge than the heat. "You've got, like, a 20 minute period when you're not feeling like your lungs are going to collapse, and after that you're pretty much on your deathbed," said Taylor. While shooting this video, Taylor found out she was nominated for a Teen Choice Award for Choice Breakout Artist.

DID YOU NOTICE?: The sun is quite a bit lower when Taylor runs to her Romeo in the field than "seconds" before when she's waiting in the castle. That's because the field wasn't actually in front of the castle. The castle scenes were shot at Castle Gwynn in Arrington-Triune, Tennessee, and the field was a car-ride away, which meant the crew raced to finish filming the field scene before sunset.

"WHITE HORSE"

THE CONCEPT: In this moody video, Taylor cries alone in a dark room, remembering both the good times she had with her ex and the worst moment — when she found out that he had another girlfriend. In the end, she decides he doesn't deserve a second chance. Taylor explains, "It's not really another 'guy cheats on me video.' You find out that I'm kind of the one that's kinda ruining the relationship without even knowing it." Once again directed by Trey Fanjoy, "White Horse" was a departure from her earlier videos. "This video is a lot different than the other videos that we've made, 'cause usually we've gone for bright colors and me looking straight to camera and singing. [This video is] a little more introspective," said Taylor.

GUEST STARRING: The heartbreaker-du-jour in "White Horse" is Stephen Colletti, best known for *Laguna Beach* and *One Tree Hill*. Explaining her choice, Taylor noted, "He had sort of the look we were going for . . . because the guy in the video is supposed to look really sweet and someone who just looks like he would never lie to you. But in the video, he does."

DID YOU NOTICE?: During her crying scene, there are two horse figurines in the room with Taylor — one on the amp beside her and one on the mantle. The restaurant scene was shot at the Mad Platter restaurant in Nashville.

"YOU BELONG WITH ME"

THE CONCEPT: Taylor's got a split personality in this video, playing both the mean girl brunette cheerleader and the literal girl-next-door, who are competing for the attention of the high school football star. The leading man and Taylor exchange proto text messages through their bedroom windows, but it's not until a made-over Taylor appears at prom that they have the courage to share their "I love you" notes.

GUEST STARRING: Lucas Till plays the hunk-next-door; he's best known for playing Miley's flame in *Hannah Montana: The Movie*. There's another guest star in this video who is less recognizable: Taylor's body double, Kelly, who helped out with those scenes where Taylor had to be in two places at once. "You Belong with Me" also saw Taylor's band suit up and join the action once again, this time as fellow band geeks.

FUN FACTS: "You Belong with Me" was shot at Pope John Paul II High School in Hendersonville where lil' bro Austin Swift was a student. The high school supplied some prom-goers (their actual prom was the night after the shoot) and helped fill the bleachers at the football game. The "Junior Jewels" T-shirt Taylor is wearing is a loaner from Caitlin Evanson, Taylor's fiddler. It's signed by Caitlin's band camp friends. It's also a popular do-it-yourself costume for fans attending Taylor's concerts. The periodic table shirt?

Lucas Till admitted that he was "crushing on Taylor for a while," so he must have been thrilled to play the object of her affection in "You Belong with Me."

That's Taylor's own contribution to the wardrobe. Director Roman White was thrilled with Taylor's portrayal of the mean cheerleader: "I think Taylor had a blast playing two very different roles. The weirdest part was that she really CHANGED once that wig went on. She walked differently. She spoke differently. She even had some fantastic new evil looks she'd toss around. It was GREAT!"

DID YOU NOTICE?: Even though Taylor's wearing giant glasses, she's the one who can see clearly in this video. Taylor needs prescription lenses in real life, though she usually opts for contacts over her black square-framed eyewear.

"FIFTEEN"

THE CONCEPT: Most of "Fifteen" takes place in a sort of dream world as Taylor looks back on her high school years. Director Roman White, who also directed "You Belong with Me," explains, "I wanted to do something different from what Taylor had done before. We wanted to take this one outside of high school. The idea is that there's a place where you can go back and revisit your memories. She's in this void and memories are manifesting around her. The story evolves and she walks across this dream world. When she walks through those doors and people fade in and out, she just has this amazing sense of innocence." Taylor exits the dream world at the very end of the video when she stands outside the high school, watching the new girls who the advice in this song is for.

GUEST STARRING: Abigail Anderson is becoming a regular in Taylor Swift videos, though this appearance is special, since she's named in the song and is the focus of the video for a verse.

TAYLOR'S HOME VIDEOS

For three of her songs, Taylor didn't turn to the professionals, but dove into her own video footage to create something all her own.

"I'm Only Me When I'm with You" is a video Taylor edited herself as a gift to her fans while they waited for the "Picture to Burn" video to come out. It's full of candid shots, goofy driving moments, and intimate performance scenes. It showcases many of Taylor's loved ones including Kellie Pickler, Abigail Anderson, Faith Hill and Tim McGraw, the Swift family, her band, and an adorable orange kitten.

"Beautiful Eyes" was included on Taylor's 2008 EP, *Beautiful Eyes*. Featuring footage from her 18th birthday party, fans got a peek at the special video montage Taylor's parents made for her as well as clips of the birthday girl celebrating with her closest friends.

"The Best Day" video was a Christmas gift for her mother, Andrea. Taylor chose her footage carefully, with the pictures taking cues from the song. It's especially neat to hear Taylor sing, "There is a video I found from back when I was three / You set up a paint set in the kitchen and you're talking to me," and to see the actual video she's singing about.

FUN FACTS: Almost the entire video was shot in front of a green screen, making it a real test of Taylor's acting abilities. About Nashville native Roman White, Taylor says, "He is hilarious. He is just walking around making jokes, cracking people up the entire time."

"CHANGE"

THE CONCEPT: "Change" is Taylor's first performance-only video (meaning there's no storyline at all), but when NBC broadcast the video, it was spliced with clips of the 2008 U.S. Olympians who had stories all their own.

GUEST STARRING: Taylor's band is back, doing that they do best.

FUN FACTS: The setting for the video is the Scottish Rite Cathedral in Indianapolis, Indiana.

DID YOU NOTICE?: Taylor wears two white dresses in this video, bringing the total number of white dresses she wears in her videos to six.

"FEARLESS"

THE CONCEPT: The video is a whirlwind look at the Fearless Tour that combines key concert moments with backstage, rehearsal, and meet-and-greet footage and has an old-style film projector quality.

GUEST STARRING: Beyond Taylor's Fearless Tour crew, her fans are the stars of this video featured in shots of her thrilled audiences and in footage of the signs, clothes, and jewelry fans make to celebrate their love of Taylor.

FUN FACTS: The director of this video, Todd Cassetty, had worked with Taylor before; he put together the enhanced CD features for *Fearless: Platinum Edition*.

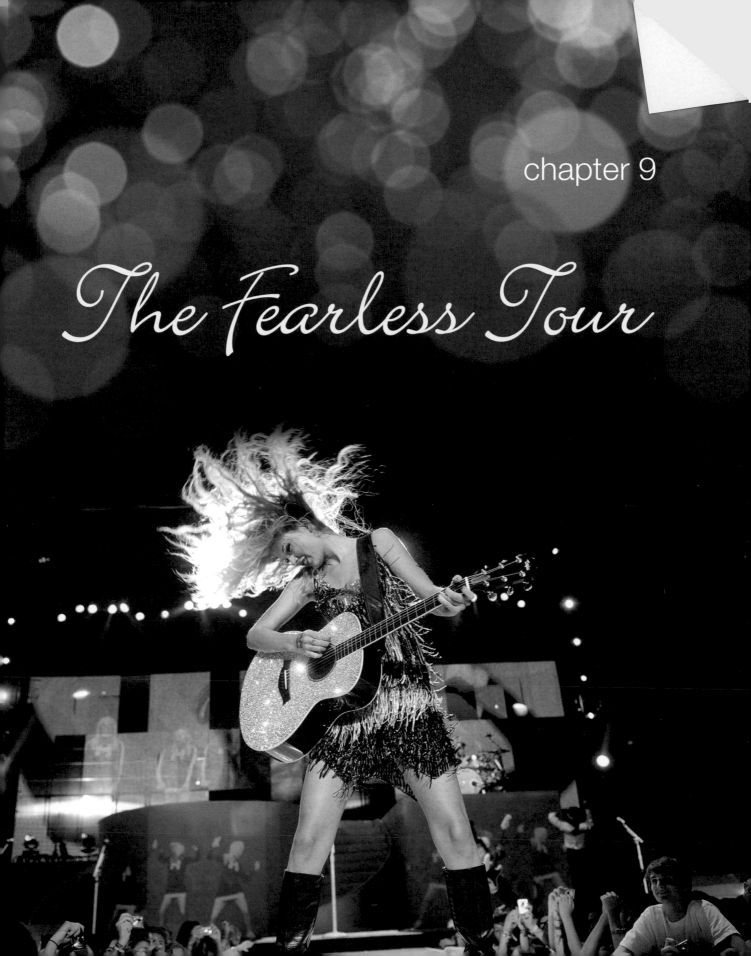

chapter 9

The Fearless Tour

With two platinum albums, singles burning up the charts, and numerous award nominations, there was only one thing missing from Taylor's swift rise to superstardom — a headlining tour. It's not that she hadn't already thought about it; she'd been dreaming about it since she was just a kid. But the clear-headed businesswoman in her realized it was best to wait until she could realize all her big ideas before embarking on the tour. "I never wanted to go into an arena and have to downsize it so there were only 5,000 or 4,000 people there," said Taylor. "So we waited a long time to make sure the headlining tour was everything I wanted the headlining tour to be."

Downsizing wouldn't be necessary. On January 30, 2009, Taylor announced a 52-city headlining tour. The Fearless Tour would start in Evansville, Indiana, and make its way all over America. "Headlining my own tour is a dream come true. This way I can play more music every night than I ever have before," said Taylor in her press release. "Having written my own songs, they are all stories in my head, and my goal for this tour is to bring those stories to life."

The tour was a dream come true for fans as well who rushed out to buy tickets, which sold out within minutes of going on sale. The nearly 40,000 tickets for her show at Madison Square Garden were snapped up within a minute, and the 20,000 for the Staples Center in L.A. within two. It was a surreal experience for Taylor, who, like any artist doing her first headlining tour, was worried about filling seats. She remembers, "The moment I knew I was having a good year was when I got a phone call from the promoter of my tour. He said, 'I'm about to put your tickets on sale for the first date of your tour.' And I was like, 'Okay, well, let me know tonight how we're doing.' I got a call from him three minutes later saying, 'You sold it out.'"

This unimaginable success was a complete shock to the rising star who confessed, "What I never expected was going out on my first headlining tour and never having to worry about ticket sales. I look at things from a practical place and a very realistic place. I've always had crazy dreams, but I've never expected them to come true."

Taylor Made

Like many musicians, Taylor had been dreaming of her ideal headlining tour for years. She'd been inspired by the artists she'd toured with — Rascal Flatts, Brad Paisley, Tim McGraw and Faith Hill, George Strait, and Kenny Chesney — and noted, "I've been on tour with every single one of my heroes, and I've seen what they do live. Some things have blown me away, and I've taken away some things that I really want to incorporate." Taylor combined what she'd learned from her idols with the plans she'd long had in the making. Many hours had been spent deciding exactly how she wanted things to look and how they would run. She told *Dateline*, "This is absolutely my baby, it's my obsession, it's the thing that I've wanted to do since I was really little, and I've been opening up for people since I was 16, so that's been a long time for me to sit there in my tour bus at night and think what would I do if I actually got to do this?"

Taylor's plans were marked by a theatrical flair likely left over from her community theater days. She told *Rolling Stone*, "I feel like there's drama that I've always been attracted to — sort of a theatrical type, dramatic performance that I feel is sometimes missing when you see shows these days. I never want people to think that they're just seeing a show where I'm playing song after song after song. When I play a song, I want people to feel like they're experiencing exactly what I went through when I wrote the song as I'm singing it for them."

What kind of theatrics did Taylor dream up? First of all, she wanted to be able to project images onto the entire stage so that what

people saw would be changing all the time. It was an uncommon feature for a country music tour, but to Taylor it was important that "you're never really seeing the same thing visually." The stage also featured a giant screen to play videos like her star-studded "Fearless Is" video and smoke machines to add the necessary moodiness to numbers like "You're Not Sorry." She also ensured that the set was rigged with an elevator to make a dramatic entrance. Some of the numbers also had elaborate sets and costumes. For the opening song, "You Belong with Me," Taylor and her band and dancers dressed up in band uniforms, and midway through, Taylor's was ripped off to reveal a trademark sparkly dress. During "Love Story," the singer and her dancers donned period costumes, and the entire stage was made to look like a castle. She tossed red chairs in "Forever & Always," and in "Should've Said No" she and Caitlin had a furious drum battle before the song ended with the onstage rain shower that got so much attention at the 2008 ACM Awards. Taylor was also sure to have multiple stage areas so that she could perform all over the arena, even out among the audience. She had up to eight costume changes, some of which take place in front of the crowd! She confesses, "I live for an onstage costume change." Her most dramatic one? A Cinderella-like transition from Renaissance ball gown to wedding dress during "Love Story." Bass player Amos Heller summed the whole production up well: "Anything Taylor wants to happen, happens onstage."

As with everything in her career, Taylor supervised all of the tour preparations from set design to selecting her six dancers. Andrea Swift explained, "Every single decision that's made, whether it's talking about artwork that's going to go on the side of the buses for the tour or a script that needs to be read, you know, almost invariably, someone in the room says, 'Have you checked with Taylor?'" It's a point Taylor isn't ashamed to admit: "I absolutely want to have my hands on everything that has to do with my career."

Yet even though she has total control, Taylor makes sure that she doesn't act like a self-righteous dictator. "There are times when you get frustrated, but the one thing you always focus on is treating people well. You just cannot storm off and freak out. People don't take you seriously if you scream, if you raise your voice, especially when you're a 19-year-old girl," she told *Dateline*.

When all the sets were built, the costumes selected, and the dancers cast, there was still a ton of rehearsing to do before this Taylor-made production was ready to hit the road. Taylor's team rented a warehouse in Nashville where the entire set was erected for three weeks of rehearsals prior to the opening show. "We've got my whole stage set up and have been rehearsing all day, every day. It's like camp. But better," Taylor blogged. "I'm in

THE FEARLESS SET LIST

For those who couldn't get tickets in time, here's the set list from the October 1, 2009, show in Pittsburgh, PA, at the Mellon Arena:

1. "You Belong with Me"
2. "Our Song"
3. "Tell Me Why"
4. "Teardrops on My Guitar"
5. "Fearless"
6. "Forever & Always"
7. "Hey Stephen"
8. "Fifteen"
9. "Tim McGraw"
10. "White Horse"
11. "Love Story"
12. "The Way I Loved You"
13. "You're Not Sorry"
14. "What Goes Around"
    (cover of Justin Timberlake's song)
15. "Picture to Burn"
16. "I'm Only Me When I'm with You"
    (with Kellie Pickler and Gloriana)
17. "Should've Said No"

heaven right now. Constantly having meetings with the video crew and the lighting guys and the carpenters and the band and running through things over and over and over again." After rehearsals in Nashville, the crew moved to Evansville, Indiana, the site of the first show, for a few days of rehearsals there.

Not all of the preparations were for the stage; Taylor made sure that the backstage area

MEET THE AGENCY

After Taylor's band filmed the video for "Picture to Burn," they adopted the nickname "The Agency." Meet the agents in Taylor's family away from home.

Al Wilson (bandleader and drums): With a rock, R&B, and Latin jazz background, Al brings a broad musical sensibility to the band. He's been playing with Taylor since he met her in 2006: "As soon as I met her, she has an electricity, an innate sense of rock about her that was cool." Of the band's sound, he told *Dateline*, "This particular 'country pop' band is more rock. It's pretty rock." For a guy who used to go to New York Rangers games at the stadium, playing Madison Square Garden on the Fearless Tour was the pinnacle of his career thus far.

Amos Heller (bass): Amos has been playing bass since he was a 10-year-old in Virginia. In 2005, after a decade of working in the Cincinnati music scene, Amos moved to Nashville and joined Taylor's band while they were on the Brad Paisley tour in late 2007. The thing that impresses Amos the most about Taylor is how she's gone above and beyond what fans would be satisfied with for this tour: "It speaks to her ambition as a performer that she doesn't just want to stand there and play the songs and there you go and goodnight, she wants to *show* people what she means by the songs."

Caitlin Evanson (fiddle, guitar, vocals): Seattle-born Caitlin is a solo artist in her own right. Classically trained in violin, she heard Pearl Jam's "Jeremy" and a whole new world of music opened up to her. She's been in a number of bands since her teen years; Caitlin says she's "always been wired to entertain." It's certainly true of her fiercely energetic perform-ances with Taylor whether she's fiddling, providing vocals, or battling it out on the drums. Caitlin wrote, "Our Taylor has included us [the band], recognized and pushed us to the front, right next to her to be a part of every award she has won this year. CMAs, VMAs, AMAs, ACMs, and pretty much any three-letter ceremonies. I feel like we've lived a thousand life-times this year alone. She loves us like family."

Grant Mickelson (lead guitar, vocals): Originally from Iowa, Grant moved to Texas to study music then to Nashville where he worked with other country music artists before joining Taylor's band in 2007. He brings a rock 'n' roll background to his playing, and is grateful to Taylor for allowing him and the band that outlet: "She's not afraid to jump to different gen-res and music." Through the experiences he's had playing with Taylor, Grant's "dreams have already happened. I have to come up with more dreams. I can't believe I get to do this."

An overwhelmed Taylor is joined onstage by her band at the CMA Awards where she won 2009's Entertainer of the Year. (L to R) Liz Huett, Caitlin Evanson, Paul Sidoti, Grant Mickelson, Amos Heller, and Al Wilson.

Liz Huett (backup vocals): Californian Elizabeth Huett first came to mainstream notice as one of the finalists on 2008's *Dance War: Bruno vs. Carrie Ann* but she made an impression on Taylor long before that. Shortly after "Tim McGraw" was released, Liz lined up to introduce herself to Taylor at a meet-and-great and asked the singer for advice on how to break into the music industry. About a year later Liz met the star again while working for an L.A. country radio station. When she finally moved to Nashville, Liz auditioned to be Taylor's backup singer and couldn't be happier that she landed the gig. Liz admires Taylor's integrity and creativity as an artist: "I'll be a fan forever and it's just so fun to be onstage rocking out with her."

Mike Meadows (banjo, guitar, mandolin, keyboard): The self-described "songwriter / performer / producer / cellist / guitarist / bassist / singer" joined Taylor's band for the Fearless Tour, and also works and records with Josh Gracin, the Pat McGee Band, MoneyPenny, and Tailgate South. While on the road with the tour, flying from Australia to Japan, he tweeted, "We are all in shock that this is our lives."

Paul Sidoti (guitar, backup vocals): Ohio native Paul started playing guitar at age five and hasn't stopped. Performing in bands in his teens, he began writing and recording music and, after college, moved to Nashville in 2000. Paul joined The Agency just after "Teardrops on My Guitar" was released. A songwriter himself, Paul says of Taylor, "The first and most important thing about her is that she's a great writer. . . . She's walked into a sound check and starting playing a song, and we're like, 'That's amazing. What is that?' and she's like, 'I'm just making it up.'" Encouraging his Twitter followers to watch the "Fearless" video, Paul wrote, "Yes . . . we are having THAT much fun. I love my job."

would be memorable as well. The "T Party" room became a backstage oasis for the performers while they were getting ready for a show, and a cool place for the band to bring fans after the show. Like everything else with the tour, Taylor oversaw the details for the Moroccan themed–room from fabric swatches to the candles Taylor had to hide from the fire marshal. Describing it, Taylor noted, "It looks nothing like backstage. It looks like your living room. The walls are covered in magenta/maroon/gold/purple draped fabric, and the floors are carpeted with oriental rugs on top. There are lanterns hanging from the ceiling and candles everywhere." The room is also equipped with a flatscreen-TV entertainment center, giant couches for napping, a foosball table, and a ping pong table. Taylor's also found a way to keep all her loved ones with her on the road: one area in the T Party room is covered with pictures of her family, Abigail

Anderson, Selena Gomez, Kellie Pickler, and the band. "It just makes me smile to have little reminders of where you come from," says Taylor.

What better way to feel at home on the road than to bring one of your best friends with you? Another important part of tour planning is selecting an opening act, and for the Fearless Tour the singer's real-life bestie Kellie Pickler would be kicking off the show. Having toured together before, opening for Brad Paisley, Taylor knew that her headlining tour would be that much better with Kellie at her side. Taylor relates, "[We're] almost like sisters at this point. She and I will sit in the dressing room 'til 2 or 3 a.m. just talking and painting our nails. It's so much fun to just have another person out on tour with you that you know you're so close with and you've known for a really long time to the point where you really just feel like they're family."

FEARLESS PRANKSTERS

Taylor and her team's endless preparation means the Fearless Tour runs like a well-oiled machine, but she's still willing to shake things up a bit with some unscheduled hijinks. "We welcome pranking. We almost require it," Taylor told the *Star-Tribune*.

During the final show on the first leg of the tour, T-Swizzle brought some hip hop to Gloriana's country act, sending her dancers out for an impromptu dance party while the band performed. Kellie Pickler couldn't escape the pranking either when the dancers appeared in butterfly and cat costumes. But Taylor had more up her sleeve. When Kellie launched into "Red High Heels," Taylor's male crew members hit the stage dressed up as women in wigs, Kellie Pickler T-shirts, and, of course, the signature red heels. Kellie got her revenge by hiding in Taylor's piano wearing a clown mask while the songstress tried to play "You're Not Sorry" and wondered why her piano sounded funny. Seems Kellie wasn't sorry for that prank! Taylor started singing "Best Days of Your Life," before hugging her pal and continuing the show.

It was during Taylor's short stint opening for Keith Urban over the summer of 2009 that she pulled off what may have been the ultimate prank. When Keith started playing his song "Kiss a Girl," Taylor and three of her band members appeared onstage in full costume and makeup as hard rock band KISS. This unscripted moment was made even sweeter for audience members when other conspirators dressed as Hershey kisses tossed the chocolates into the crowd. But Taylor was the one who was surprised when she got a tweet from the KISS member she'd impersonated: "Ace Frehley tweeted me. Oh. My God. RT @ace_frehley @taylorswift13 saw your prank on YouTube, you looked great in my outfit. ROCK N ROLL!"

Taylor signed up another opening band: four-person country music group Gloriana, who started playing together in 2008 and had a top 15 hit on the Hot Country Songs chart by February 2009. Announcing her decision to bring the band on tour, Taylor wrote, "They're AMAZING and I love their new single, 'Wild at Heart.' I heard it and immediately knew I wanted them on this tour." Not more than a year earlier, people had been saying similar things about Taylor, but now she was the one helping a new act find its audience.

Headfirst, Fearless: Opening Night

Months of preparation and years of dreaming culminated on April 23, 2009, in Evansville,

Indiana. The opening night of the Fearless Tour had finally arrived. As Team Taylor gathered in the T Party room before the show, they huddled up for one last heart-to-heart before going on stage. Bandleader and drummer Al Wilson told the group, "I want to say that I have never been so proud to be on stage with people as much as I am with you guys. I'm so proud to be a part of this. This is, tonight, officially a huge new chapter, beginning right now. Life as we know it has changed from 10 minutes from now."

Taylor thanked all the people who helped get her to this incredible moment: "I just want to say that I didn't have a senior class and I didn't have a sorority. You guys are my senior class, and you guys are my sorority, and you guys are my brothers and my sisters, and you guys are the people who are helping me become the person I'm going to be."

Clad in their "You Belong with Me" band costumes, the group marched out on stage, only to be greeted by thousands of voices screaming in unison. "When I hear that high-pitched sound of all those people screaming together, it's like I want to get on stage right now," says Taylor. She was in her element. "I love being onstage. It's one of my favorite things in the world," gushes the performer. "And on this tour, I really focused on entertaining people, doing things they wouldn't expect me to do."

The constant screaming was a good sign that the Evansville crowd was entertained. Coming off stage, dripping wet and wrapped in her purple Taylor Swift robe, Taylor gushed, "The energy was just incredible. The people were, like, freaking out, losing their minds."

She was soaked through and freezing cold — the rain at the end of "Should've Said No" wasn't heated water — but Taylor felt that stormy moment had been the best in the show: "The highlight for me was the rain . . . I've done that once at an awards show, but never in front of a concert crowd and it was so crazy. It was so much fun getting to do that."

Always the perfectionist, even after her stellar performance Taylor had elements she wanted to improve. "I have a lot of notes for lighting and stuff," she mentioned after she came offstage in Evansville. That perfectionism, applied to every possible aspect of the performance, meant that fans across America would get the fairytale performance Taylor dreamed of. Kellie Pickler sums up her bestie best: "She puts on an incredible show. Every night she puts her heart and soul into every performance. And the fans, they know that about her, so I don't think anyone's left the show disappointed."

Life on the Road

With over 50 scheduled shows in the first leg of the tour alone, Taylor had a jam-packed six months ahead. And though a rock star lifestyle may seem glamorous, Taylor's duties went far beyond putting on an incredible show every night. A regular day includes five or six interviews and a meet-and-greet session starting at 5 p.m. before the show's 8 p.m. start. She also greets winners of radio contests or people pulled from the nosebleed sections. "My brain does get fried, but I never get tired of this," she told *Women's Health*. These long days mean that Taylor's tour schedule usually

alternates between four-day runs of shows and a few days off, so she can rest and be ready to give her all in the next set of performances.

One thing that makes long stretches on the road easier is Taylor's custom-made tour bus. When she was an opening act, she shared a bus with her entire band, but now she has a bus for just her and her mom that she designed herself. It has a sitting area swathed in plum and gold–colored plush fabrics, bunk beds with fold-down flatscreen TVs, and even a working fireplace! On the door, Taylor's lucky 13 is painted and her motto stretches over an arch: "Never Never Never Give Up."

Having a seriously pimped ride makes time on the road more bearable, but Taylor's number-one comfort through long tour stretches is her mom, who's almost always by her side. She's there for a restorative ice cream binge and *Grey's Anatomy* marathon, or to offer her daughter honest feedback. "If she saw something that could have been better, she's not going to hold it in. She's not going to sugarcoat: it's total honesty," says Taylor. "She was my friend on bad days, but she'd also provide me with the accurate amount of constructive criticism." And despite her mom supervising her career, Taylor is careful to make one thing clear, "My parents are the coolest. My mother is so not a momager."

Occasionally, Taylor's father Scott joins his wife and daughter at shows, bringing his own brand of unconditional support and his great sense of humor. "He's a social butterfly, and loves being on tour. He loves it so much, he thinks it's absolutely hilarious to mess with me and try to embarrass me as much as possible," laughs Taylor.

Despite mother and daughter logging more time together on a six-month tour than most teens spend with their moms in all of high school, the two rarely bicker. "My mom and I really get along, and my dad and I get along really well so it's gotten to the point where all we argue about is stupid stuff," assures Taylor.

Life on the road may be exhausting, but Taylor, the overachiever at heart, thrives with an overloaded agenda. "I get really restless when I haven't worked for a day and a half," she admits. "I have a recurring dream that people are lined up next to my bed, waiting for autographs and taking pictures of me." It's no wonder Taylor's accomplished so much, she's even working in her sleep!

chapter 10

Beyond
the Music

As if being a multi-platinum, award-winning recording artist with a sold-out international tour wasn't impressive enough, Taylor Swift has managed to tackle even more. As 2010 approached, Taylor could add actress and avatar to her résumé.

Though she had acted in community-theater shows as a kid, Taylor's first acting jobs in front of a camera were her music videos where she'd act out the storyline of her songs alongside professional actors. She also got used to being in front of cameras during interviews, especially in-depth ones like the GAC *Shortcuts* documentary about her, and in shows like MTV's *Once Upon a Prom*. In June 2008, MTV cameras followed Taylor and Abigail as they attended prom at Hillcrest High School in Alabama. Said Taylor, "My senior year I got to go to a prom . . . and took my best friend and we both had dates we never met before. But it was fun!" Taylor loves including her bestie in her adventures and Abigail is happy to join in: "It's a great opportunity for somebody my age to just follow her. I'm not so much following in her footsteps, but just getting to experience and witness what somebody goes through when they become a celebrity or they are in the limelight. Any opportunity she gives me like that, I definitely take it." Abigail, a three-time All-American and four-time "Swimmer of the Year" at Hendersonville High, attends Kansas University where she swims on their varsity team and studies journalism. Her distance

from Hendersonville and the rigors of being a school-record-breaking varsity athlete combined with Taylor's crazy schedule means the best friends have to work hard to see each other. But their friendship is so strong that they're inseparable even when physically apart.

Taylor paired another close personal relationship with time in front of the cameras when she made her big-screen debut in *Jonas Brothers: The 3D Concert Experience*, which was released in theaters in February 2009. She was pretty familiar with her role: she played herself and sang "Should've Said No" with the brothers Jonas. At the time, she was dating Joe Jonas, about whom "Forever & Always" was later written. The two had decided not to go public with their relationship though gossip columnists correctly pegged the pair as a couple. It was only after the infamous 27-second phone call during which Joe broke up with Taylor that she decided it was open season; she discussed the breakup on *Ellen*, and posted a comical video telling a Taylor Swift doll to stay away from a Joe Jonas doll.

Taylor didn't let a bad breakup keep her down when she had another milestone right around the corner. A natural onscreen, Taylor had said she was "definitely open to acting roles; it just depends on the story." She didn't have to wait long for the right role to be offered to her. A huge fan of *CSI* ("I like intense shows about intense things"), Taylor was over the moon when she was cast as murder victim Haley Jones in the episode "Turn, Turn, Turn," which aired on March 5, 2009. Her episode drew a season-high viewership of almost 21 million people.

She was back on the big screen in April, working with another one of her best friends, Miley Cyrus, in *Hannah Montana: The Movie*. In a cameo appearance, Taylor played the unnamed girl singing in the barn; the song she sang was "Crazier," which appeared on the

TAYLOR'S TOP TRACKS

- "If Ever I Could Love," by Keith Urban: Taylor named this her favorite song at the end of 2009.

- "The Tracks of My Tears," by Smokey Robinson and the Miracles: Her dad "used to play lots of Motown songs on our summer vacations."

- "What Goes Around" by Justin Timberlake: Taylor loves this song so much she sings it in concert.

- "Umbrella," Rihanna: Another favorite to cover, Taylor's version appeared on her *iTunes Live from SoHo* album.

- "Fist City," Loretta Lynn: She loves the line, "I'm not saying my baby's a saint, 'cause he ain't."

- "Taylor," Jack Johnson: This song was T-Swift's ringtone; she chooses to ignore what the song's Taylor does for a living, instead pretending it's about her.

- "Lose Yourself," Eminem: A surprising choice to cover in concert, Taylor loves this inspirational track that echoes her motto to "never, never, never give up."

- "Hysteria," Def Leppard: Taylor was blown away when she got to perform with her mom's favorite group in 2008.

- "Thinking of You," Katy Perry: Taylor is happy to count Katy as one of her good friends and really admires her songwriting.

- "Nothing Compares 2 U," Sinead O'Connor: Taylor thinks this is one of the most beautiful songs ever composed.

movie's soundtrack. Taylor is close pals with Miley (who also spends time near Nashville at her parents' home in Franklin) along with two other "Disney girls," Demi Lovato and Selena Gomez. Says Taylor, "It's really awesome to get to hang out with those girls and to call them friends." Sometimes she forgets the age difference between them: "I feel like Miley, Selena, and Demi are my age. It's crazy." The girls may not always get to see one other with their busy lifestyles but they are always there for each other. Before Miley's AMA performance, which happened to be on her birthday, Taylor and the girls arranged for a big birthday cake backstage to surprise her. For Demi's birthday, Taylor gave her mace, "because I

"It was really neat. Total blonde power. After the game, we pulled into a gas station and Carrie saw this guy talking to Taylor. We were like, This isn't right! I said, 'Get away from her, you old man. If you're still around when we finish filling up with gas, we'll make a hood ornament out of you!'" — Kellie Pickler on a girls' night out at a hockey game with Taylor and Carrie Underwood.

don't want anything to happen to [her]. Demi loved it, and her dad loved it too." Taylor and Selena talk on the phone every day, as do Taylor and actress Emma Stone (*Zombieland*).

In the first week of November 2009, some of those phone calls must have been about Taylor's upcoming appearance as host and musical guest on the legendary sketch

Taylors Swift and Lautner film a scene in *Valentine's Day*.

comedy show *Saturday Night Live*. Back in January, she had been the youngest country artist to be the musical guest, and that experience landed in Taylor's top three "pinch-yourself" moments. As host of the November 7th episode, she appeared in numerous skits and performed two songs; some of her more memorable moments included playing Bella in a *Twilight* parody (where the dreamy vampire was replaced by a less-than-dreamy Frankenstein monster) and her "Monologue Song (La La La)," where she mocked her music, her love of all things sparkly, and the Kanye West incident at the 2009 MTV VMAs.

The other hot topic in her monologue was her rumored relationship with *Twilight* actor Taylor Lautner. The two met while filming the

Taylor and her dear friend Selena Gomez at the Hope for Haiti Now telethon on January 22, 2010. Says Taylor of Selena: "It is very easy for girls to get caught up in Hollywood and the spotlight, and they become different. And I feel like the people that I've been lucky to meet and be friends with are still really real people."

star-studded romantic comedy *Valentine's Day*. That film, directed by Garry Marshall, was Taylor's official big-screen acting debut and her plot line involved a romance with the other Taylor. It was confusing for the crew to have two Taylors on set, so girl Taylor suggested that instead she be called "Swiftie" (her band's nickname for her). Once the cameras stopped rolling, the two Taylors continued to spend time together. They were spotted at a hockey game and out for dinner, but neither officially confirmed their relationship. Before the media had settled on a cutesy name for them (Taylor Squared?), the romance had cooled off. But their friendship continued with each warmly describing the other as amazing. Always a class act, Taylor Swift showed her support for Taylor Lautner by giving him a standing ovation when he won a 2010 People's Choice Award. In Japan on Valentine's Day 2010, Swiftie missed the premiere of *Valentine's Day* but her song on its soundtrack, "Today Was a Fairytale," didn't miss the mark at all. It became her highest debut on the Billboard Hot 100 at number two.

With television and film credits now on her list of accomplishments, Taylor got into the gaming universe when the creators of *Guitar Hero* approached her to be a part of their spin-off project, *Band Hero*, which was released in November 2009. Performing "Love Story," "You Belong with Me," and "Picture to Burn," a digital version of Taylor, modeled on real-life Taylor, appears onstage with "magical sparkles" swirling around her. Taylor advises people to do some neck exercises before playing her avatar since there's a lot of hair swinging going on in her performance. Joked Taylor, "Hair as well as guitar are the instruments that I use."

There's no end to the opportunities being offered to the superstar. Taylor picked up a gig as an NHL spokesperson, appearing in commercials for the Nashville Predators. Like everything else in her career, Taylor only agreed to do it because it's something she actually loves. When she has time off, she often heads to a Predators game. She also loves baking, and is slowly becoming a better cook, learning her mother's recipes (and writing them down in a little red book). Whether she's having a low-key dinner with Paramore's Hayley Williams, chatting on the phone with one of her best friends in L.A., or driving around and talking about boys with Abigail, Taylor's life outside of the public eye is all about the simple yet rewarding moments spent with the people she loves.

Taylor Nation

Taylor Swift remembers what it was like to be a fan who idolized country singers. She once waited in line for hours to get LeAnn Rimes' autograph and she owns a life-size Brad Paisley stand-up poster. She admits that even now that she has reached celebrity status, "I get starstruck all the time. I ask for autographs at award shows like a superfan." That's

There are lots of celebrities who take the time to stop for an autograph or a quick hello, but there are very few people willing to put on an impromptu show. Luckily for her fans, Taylor is one of them.

One day at the Nashville airport while Taylor and her band were waiting for a flight, some fans approached the local celebrity and asked her to play a song. Taylor told *Allure*, "They saw my guitar sitting there. So I got my band members to bust out their guitars too, and we just played a concert at the terminal. It's so much fun doing stuff like that."

On another occasion, Taylor and her band stopped into a Fresno, California, ice cream shop for a sweet treat and discovered that the woman working at the register was a huge T-Swift fan. That fan got a treat of her own when the band brought in their instruments and put on a private show right there in the shop! In an interview with the local paper, Taylor explained, "When people tell me they like my music, they have no idea how good that makes me feel. I take every opportunity I can to make it up to them."

part of the reason she treats her fans well, but the other reason is the obvious one — she wouldn't be where she is today without them. They buy her concert tickets and albums, request her songs on the radio, and help her win fan-voted awards like American Music Awards, Teen Choice Awards, and CMT Music Awards.

For some celebrities, fans are just faceless screaming masses, and they treat them that way. But Taylor gives her fans all the respect they deserve as people, and tries to make each fan encounter special. "If I sign an autograph for someone, I don't put them in the category of 'fan' and keep them at arm's length," she told *Self*. "If we strike up a conversation and we like the same things and we have the same sense of humor, then they're my friend. It doesn't matter how I met them."

— *love love love T* —

One of the earliest ways Taylor interacted with her fans was through MySpace. Many musicians make MySpace pages with the express purpose of promoting their work; Taylor made hers just because "all my friends had MySpaces, and that's how they talked to each other. So I wanted to be cool too, and I wanted to make a MySpace." As an aspiring musician it was only natural for her to post music, and soon enough her talent spread like wildfire. MySpace was one of the first and easiest ways for new listeners to hear her music. She told CMT, "That was not a clever scheme. That was an accident . . . I didn't expect for MySpace to be a thing that propelled my career or was this huge army that it's become."

What Taylor values most about MySpace is the chance to directly communicate with her fans who tell her how her music affects them. Andrea Swift told GAC, "They come on and tell their life story and why the song has meant so much to them and that's where it becomes a real personal thing. They're sharing. They're sharing their lives with Taylor." The reason fans feel comfortable sharing their lives with Taylor is that she's also sharing her life with them.

As she started recording her first album, Taylor also began posting blogs about her experience. Her posts make up a candid, funny, and inspiring story that allows fans to share those moments. Taylor may write about an awards ceremony or her snoring cat, but the blend of insight into the music business and average-girl details make Taylor's journey all the more compelling and real. Even if she has a swanky tour bus and more money than most people will see in their lifetime, she still acts like the girl-next-door. She told *Glamour*, "I've never felt like I needed to tone down being seen as a regular person."

Taylor gave her fans even more insight into her world when she started posting videos on MySpace as well. The videos are a kind of all-access pass that invites fans right into Taylor's home or car or backstage at a show. It's exhilarating to be able to share in the joy of moments like Taylor's reaction to earning four CMA Award nominations. While so many other celebrities only present a carefully polished public persona, Taylor shows her true face — even if it's not wearing any makeup. The videos are compilations Taylor edits herself (and often she's the camera

operator too) and her do-it-yourself spirit lets fans get to know her even more through the goofy footage she chooses or the songs she plays in the background.

As much as Taylor gives on MySpace, she gets back in the wonderful comments from fans. She reveals, "Going on MySpace immediately makes my day better. I may be thinking, 'My hair doesn't look right,' 'I don't like this outfit,' or 'I need to do this or that,' but when I log in, they're like, 'Your music has changed my life,' 'Your music got me through this breakup,' 'Your song means so much to me.' When people are constantly being loving to you, it's the nicest thing. It's just so cool. It's a constant stream of love."

Whenever she has the time, Taylor tries to reply and have a conversation with her fans. "I spend a lot of time [responding] to fan emails. It's really, really important to me to make sure people know that I love them, I appreciate them, and I'm nothing without them. I'll never forget about them," says the star. "I'll always be on MySpace as much as I possibly can, trying to get back to them. Sometimes I get so addicted to it that I can't stop commenting people back. There's always one more that's so sweet. I've stayed up all night doing it."

With over 1.8 million friends, over 775,000 comments, and over 111 million profile views, Taylor Swift is a MySpace success story. So much so that when the site launched MySpace Music, Taylor joined MySpace CEO Chris DeWolfe for the celebration on *Today*. But the real reason Taylor's been so successful goes beyond any website. At the end of her very personal MySpace profile introduction, Taylor takes the time to show her connection to the people who have helped her make her dreams come true: "I'm a fan of fans. You are absolutely wonderful to me. I've got your back, just like you've had mine. To anyone who has gone out and bought my CD, or come to a show, or even turned my song up when it came on the radio, all I can say is thank you."

SuperStar

Taylor remembers the first time she was recognized. It was July 27, 2006; "Tim McGraw" was her only song on the radio; and she was in the Boise, Idaho, airport when a woman approached her and said, "Taylor, I just love your song and want to wish you great things in your career." The young songstress thought the lady had been sent over by her mom or her label rep, but she knew Taylor from the radio and her just-released video. Taylor blogged, "This was the first time someone had actually KNOWN who I was and MY NAME. Wow. I just walked over and hugged her, and said . . . 'You're the first person who's ever done that, thank you.' It was an amazing moment to remember, and I always will."

Before long, anonymity would be a thing of the past as the golden-haired beauty could be spotted on TV and in magazines. Whether she's shopping or eating in a restaurant, people gravitate toward her, and Taylor always takes time out for her fans. This could get frustrating, but unlike some celebrities who constantly gripe about the high price of fame, the young country artist acknowledges that she knew what she was getting into when she started her career. Taylor told *Marie Claire*, "When you spend so much time daydreaming

about things like [being recognized], when that actually happens you don't ever complain about it. When I go to a restaurant, yeah I know that a line is probably going to form in front of the table, but didn't I always wish for that? Yeah, I did. So it's like, I never want to be the girl who wanted something so bad her whole life and then gets it and complains about it. I'm not going to be that girl."

Taylor also gets that her celebrity status is something *she* signed up for, not her friends. "I'll find out that a group of my friends went out to dinner," says Taylor, "but they wanted it to be a low-key night and not worry about people coming up to the table every other second and asking for autographs, so they didn't invite me. I can understand that."

Luckily since she lives in Nashville, Taylor is not plagued by the paparazzi as much as some of her friends in L.A. are. But when Taylor ends up in the City of Angels, she handles the intrusive photographers like a pro. She usually just ignores them, though she can't help noticing some of life's funny coincidences. One day she tweeted, "There's nothing quite like singing along in the car to @ladygaga 'paparazzi' while actually being chased by paparazzi."

Maybe part of the reason Taylor isn't too bothered by the paparazzi is that she never gives them any scandalous photos to sell. Unlike some infamous stars who lose themselves on the rollercoaster ride to the top, Taylor isn't caught up in the party scene. And it's not because she's forced to behave by her parents or management — she makes responsible decisions on her own. "It's not like I've been beaten down by some corporation that's

forcing me to always behave myself — I just naturally do," Taylor explained. "Sometimes people are fascinated by the fact that I don't care about partying, almost to the point where they think it's weird. I think when we get to the point where it's strange for you to not be stumbling around high on something at 19, it's a warped world." With a star that's rising higher every day, Taylor's not about to let herself get distracted. "My career is the only thing I think about. It's stronger than any alcohol, stronger than any drug, stronger than anything else you could try — so why should I do those things, you know?" Instead, Taylor's found a more constructive way to rebel, and she insists, "For me, rebelling is done with words."

Beyond what's best for her career, Taylor also thinks about what's best for her fans. With millions of young people looking up to her, she wants to set the best example possible. She explains, "Every time I'm faced with a decision or a choice, I think about the six-year-old girl in the front row of my concert, and what she'd think about it. Then I think about her mom, and what she'd think. I never lose sight of what's really important. To me, it's those girls."

Being a role model isn't just about staying away from alcohol and drugs, it's also about how she chooses to present herself. She's arrived at photo shoots and requested new wardrobe options that would provide her with a bit more coverage. "I've gotten there and they had a wardrobe rack and the only things hanging on the wardrobe racks were bras and bustiers," she told the *Tennessean*. "I'm like, 'Cool. Where are the clothes?' 'Those are the clothes.' 'No, no, no. Let's get clothes. I wear clothes.'"

Despite the media badgering her to reveal intimate details about her personal life, she fends them off by replying, "It's fine to talk about love publicly. But I think when you talk about virginity and sex publicly, people just automatically picture you naked. And as much as I can prevent people picturing me naked, I'm going to."

And while it's good that Taylor isn't a regular in the celebrity scandal sheets, her real value as a role model comes from her insistence on treating others well, her gratitude for what she has, and her single-minded determination to pursue her dream, no matter how impossible it may seem.

Blonde Ambition

chapter 12

In a 2007 interview with *Florida Entertainment Scene*, Taylor was asked where she thought she'd be in five years. The rising star replied, "In five years, I'll be 22. I'd really like to be starting to headline. I think that would be amazing. I'd love to have another platinum album, and I'd love to have won some sort of award (an ACM or CMA, I don't care). Five years is a long time, so who knows what might happen. I never thought all of this would happen in one year, so I can't wait to see my life in five!"

As it turned out, Taylor's career was in fast-forward, and she wouldn't have to wait five years for any of those dreams to come true.

And the Award Goes to . . .

Taylor's talents have been recognized at nearly every music award ceremony in America — the ACM Awards, the CMA Awards, the CMT Music Awards, the AMAs, and the Grammys. Her pop success also ensured her a place at the MTV Video Awards, the People's Choice Awards, the Teen Choice Awards, and the Kids' Choice Awards. She's become a regular feature on the red carpet and onstage, where she routinely surprises fans with collaborations (with Def Leppard or T-Pain) and unexpected theatrics (such as the pouring rain shower at the 2008 ACM Awards).

After less than two years on the scene, the young songstress was taking home some of the industry's most prestigious awards. At the 2009 Academy of Country Music Awards, she took home not only Album of the Year for *Fearless* but also the Crystal Milestone Award, which recognizes the most country albums

sold that year. Back in 2007, the Country Music Association had earmarked Taylor as promising new talent in country music by giving her the Horizon Award. Just two years later, the CMA confirmed their prediction. At the ceremony in November 2009, Taylor took home Album of the Year and three other awards, though all of those were eclipsed by the evening's greatest honor — the Entertainer of the Year Award, previously won by artists like George Strait, Garth Brooks, Shania Twain, the Dixie Chicks, Tim McGraw, and Kenny Chesney. Taylor was the youngest person ever to win the prestigious award, and the first female solo artist to do so in almost a decade (since her hero Shania Twain in 1999). Accepting her award, which was presented to her by Faith Hill and Tim McGraw, the overcome performer gushed, "I'll never forget this moment, because at this moment everything that I have ever wanted just happened to me."

After her historic win, Taylor related to *Billboard*, "I'd have to say that was the most mind-blowing experience, hearing my name called and winning that award. That is an award I had placed in an unattainable spot in my head. To be the youngest to win it makes me love country music even more," and she notes, "We wished for this, my parents and I, every single day without actually believing it would come true."

After winning over 50 music industry awards, one still evaded the celebrated songstress: a Grammy. She'd been nominated in 2008 for Best New Artist and lost to Amy Winehouse. When the nominations for the 2010 Grammy Awards were announced,

Taylor had eight new chances to earn the coveted golden gramophone. With nominations in both country and mainstream categories, Taylor was competing against hot pop acts like Beyoncé and Lady Gaga. At the end of the night, Nashville's golden girl had proven up to the challenge. Early in the evening, the surprised young star held her first Grammy when she accepted her award for Best Female Country Vocal Performance for "White Horse," and she exclaimed, "This is my first Grammy, you guys! This is a Grammy."

Taylor became pretty familiar with the award before the evening was over. She followed with another award for "White Horse" in the category of Best Country Song; Best Country Album for *Fearless*; and most impressively, the night's most coveted award, Album of the Year. Accepting the award, the ecstatic songstress was sure to thank her parents, and collected herself to emphasize, "All of us, when we're all 80 years old and we are telling the same stories over and over again to our grandkids, and they're so annoyed with us,

this is the story we're going to be telling over and over again — in 2010, that we got to win Album of the Year at the Grammys."

Unfortunately, Taylor's Grammy glory was somewhat tainted by a critical backlash to her singing at the ceremony. Music critics noted that she was off-key during her performances, which included her new single "Today Was a Fairytale" and two collaborations with the legendary Stevie Nicks on "Rhiannon" and "You Belong with Me." Scott Borchetta came to his golden girl's defense, noting that Taylor was having technical problems that prevented her from hearing the complete vocal mix of her duet with Stevie. (Taylor was not the only performer who experienced pitch problems that night.) Scott also stated, "Maybe she's not the best technical singer, but she is the best emotional singer because everybody else who gets up there and is technically perfect, people don't seem to want more of it," adding, "No one is perfect on any given day. Maybe in that moment, we didn't have the best night, but in the same breath, maybe we did."

While *Spin* music critic Alan Light was a part of the negative chorus, he also remarked that a less-than-perfect performance is at least a guarantee of authenticity in an age when most young performers lip-synch. "The fact that it's not perfect, in some ways, has been an asset," he noted. "That makes it all the more believable, to a certain point." That said, he stressed that a performer of Taylor's celebrity needs to work on her television performances, and Scott Borchetta assured the media that Taylor would do just that. "She's a very intelligent girl," said the record executive. "She's going to keep addressing it and keep getting better." Considering Taylor's extraordinary drive and determination, there's no doubt that's true, and that Taylor has many more award wins (and fantastic performances) ahead of her.

More Fearless than Ever

After the sold-out success of her 2009 Fearless Tour, fans desperately hoped Taylor would go back on the road again soon. On October 8, 2009, Taylor had an announce-ment that would make those wishes come true — the Fearless Tour would be back in February 2010.

The tour started in the Land Down Under where Taylor played seven shows to a welcoming Aussie crowd and rave reviews. She'd visited Australia a year earlier and played in smaller venues. In 2010 she was selling out arenas with the Fearless Tour. On her blog, she recalled seeing Coldplay at Sydney's Acer Arena on her first visit and thinking, "Wouldn't it be amazing if someday down the line, we could play in this arena?" Now she notes, "Playing two nights in that arena less than a year later was something I'll never forget."

Concert-goers weren't likely to forget it either. A *Herald Sun* reviewer praised, "Her Fearless show is like watching a kid in a candy store bringing her dreams to life in her first world tour," and added, "The atmosphere was as electric as any boy band concert." *Adelaide Now* noted, "It was refreshing to witness a number-one artist dedicate her heart and soul to the delivery of her songs, rather than just her dance moves . . . and it was clear that this is a musical talent who is only at the beginning of her career." Taylor had just as much love for her host country, tweeting, "Sydney, Australia . . . You just stole my heart." As the band traveled all over the sprawling country, Taylor used her time off to see the sights, go to the beach, and (much to the chagrin of wildlife officials) feed the wild possums. It was a road trip to remember for the Fearless team. She tweeted, "My band + dancers + Gloriana + me. One bus. 2 hour drive to Newcastle. Summer camp style. Sometimes life at 20 resembles life at 10."

On Valentine's Day, Taylor jumped continents, landing in Japan to a tremendous display of love from fans. Even with a 6 a.m. arrival, she was greeted at Tokyo's Narita International Airport by 150 fans and was given a card that read, "Welcome to Japan. Congratulations on your Grammys!" No wonder she was tweeting, "Japan is amazing. Japan is amazing. Japan is amazing." Taylor played a sold-out show at Zepp Arena and discovered that the Taylor Nation spanned more continents than she'd realized. After the show she tweeted, "Wow. Just wow. Tokyo, I'll never forget that show. We'll be back soon!! The band and I can't stop smiling." In her photo blog, Taylor also noted, "Fans were so welcoming to us, everywhere we went. I loved the presents and the letters. I can't wait to go back and play more shows." During her stay, the "21st

Century Cinderella Girl" (as she was called in Japan) also found out that *Fearless* had earned its gold certification there. Not long after she arrived Taylor was saying *Sayonara* to Japan as she headed home to prepare for the 2010 North American leg of the Fearless Tour.

The North American dates started March 4, with nearly every one once again selling out (often within minutes). Kellie Pickler and Gloriana returned as opening acts. Who would pass on a chance to be part of a tour where every day was a fairytale?

Taylor's Next Chapter

"The second that I put out *Fearless*, the moment that album came out and I was done with it, I started writing for my next album," said Taylor in December 2009. "I love to plan

20 steps ahead of myself, and it's [a] really fun competition game that I play with myself, trying to top what I've done last. For this next record, that's all that I've been thinking about, that's all that my mind has been fixated on for the last year, and it's all I'm going to be thinking about for this next year."

After two multi-platinum international hit albums, fans and media alike also have the pop-country sensation's next album on their minds. While *Fearless* expanded on the pop sensibility heard on *Taylor Swift*, Taylor shows no signs of making a major departure in the sound of her next offering, especially since she was showered with awards for *Fearless*. Her pop-country fusion will likely remain for her third full-length album, but as she enters a new stage in her life, the songs may reflect that change. As Taylor told the *Reading Eagle*, "I write songs about my life. When my life changes, so will my music. It's as simple as that."

The album is expected in late 2010, two years after the release of *Fearless*. Taylor told *Rolling Stone*, "I think two years of growth and development and feelings and life intake, love intake, emotion output is my preferred formula for albums right now." Taylor loves recording, sending out enthusiastic tweets from the studio: "Studio-ness with all the same boys who played on *Fearless*. Home-made cupcakes were brought. Awkward fist-pumps happened. Onward!" and "More recording. So excited. So excited. So excited. See, I said that three times. Once for every album we've made in this studio."

Reporting on Taylor's progress, Scott Borchetta announced in February 2010, "She was on an amazing writing spree through December and January, and we were able to go in and cut all those things." But with Taylor's habit of adding songs at the last minute, the track list is far from final, and Scott added, "If she writes something great between now and July, it will go on the record. She's been extraordinarily prolific the last six months." It's no surprise, really, from an artist who claims to have written over 500 songs. As Taylor told *Rolling Stone*, "I can't stop writing songs. I can't stop. I can't turn it off." And fans can only hope she won't anytime soon.

Independent Woman

Taylor may be a fiercely independent musician, but, as a 20-year-old, she's a little behind in striking out on her own. Taylor was happy to remain in Hendersonville living with her parents for the beginning of her career, and told *People*, "[My parents] give me space, but I've still got people to talk to when I get lonely." But in September 2009 she revealed that she'd bought her first apartment — a 4,062 square foot penthouse in Nashville. Since she'd thought about becoming an interior designer when she was younger, having a blank slate of her own was a dream come true. She recalls, "I looked at this place and said, 'The view is amazing. Let's change everything else.'" Her Taylor-made changes include bright colors, handpicked antiques, and some very special custom installations, such as a giant birdcage and a pond filled with koi. Taylor told Oprah, "I love more of an old world, eclectic feel with mismatched chairs and a different knob on every cabinet."

She's catching up with her college-age

friends in terms of living arrangements, but does the singer-songwriter have any plans to enter the hallowed halls of academia herself? Not for the time being. Taylor told CMT, "Right now, I'm pursuing my career. I always thought that I would go to college, most definitely. But then I really thought about it and assessed the situation, and I can't leave this life. Going to college would mean saying goodbye to my music career, and I just can't do that. There just wouldn't be enough time in the day to be on tour, do interviews, meet-and-greets, TV appearances, and everything else that I need to do and go to college. Maybe later on in life I'll end up taking a few classes or doing it online. But right now, it just isn't where I need to be."

As for her music career, Taylor has two multi-platinum albums, a sold-out headlining tour, international success, and more awards than most artists earn in a lifetime. What other goals could she possibly have left to achieve? Taylor's just taking it one step at a time. "As soon as I accomplish one goal, I replace it with another one," she explained to VH1. "I try not to get too far ahead of myself. I just say to myself, 'All right, well, I'd like to headline a tour,' and then when I get there, we'll see what my next goal is."

It's hard to set new goals when Taylor's entire career has exceeded her wildest dreams. When Oprah asked her if her life was as she'd imagined it would be, Taylor had a simple answer: "It's better." It'll likely get better yet, for the gracious singer-songwriter's star shows no signs of fading, and with her talent, her dedication to her fans, and her tireless energy, there's no doubt that Taylor Swift's fairytale has just begun.

chapter 13

Every Day Is a Fairytale

THE TAYLOR SWIFT NEWS DIARY

EARLY 2004

★ After years of festivals, karaoke bars, and dreaming of success, Taylor is signed to a development deal with RCA. She has her foot in the door of a record company, but the deal offers no guarantee that she'll emerge with an album.

FALL 2004

★ Taylor is featured in the Abercrombie & Fitch "rising stars" national advertising campaign.

SPRING 2005

★ Taylor lands a job at Sony/ATV Publishing, which makes her the youngest staff songwriter they had ever hired.

AUGUST 2005

★ Like many people her age, Taylor takes her place on MySpace, which becomes the earliest way to hear her music, and later one of her best ways of staying connected to fans all over the world.

SEPTEMBER 2005

★ Taylor is one of the first performers signed by Scott Borchetta to his new label, Big Machine Records.

JUNE 2006

★ Taylor's first single, "Tim McGraw," hits the airwaves on the 19th, debuting at number 60 on the Hot Country Songs chart.

★ Taylor attends her first award show, the Academy of Country Music Awards in Las Vegas.

AUGUST 2006
★ Taylor makes her small-screen acting debut with her first music video, "Tim McGraw."

OCTOBER 2006
★ On October 24, 2006, Taylor releases her self-titled debut. She celebrates its launch on *Good Morning America*, which had declared her a breakout artist back in 2004. The singer is thrilled, telling GAC, "This is my chance to bring my music out of my bedroom where I'm writing it."
★ The performer joins her first major tour, opening nine shows for Rascal Flatts.

JANUARY 2007
★ *Taylor Swift* earns its gold certification (marking 500,000 albums sold).
★ The songstress hits the road with country legend George Strait.

APRIL 2007
★ Taylor attends the CMT Music Awards, where she takes home her first piece of mantel bling — "The Buckle" for Breakthrough Video of the Year for "Tim McGraw."
★ Taylor brings the Buckle on the road with her on Brad Paisley's Bonfires & Amplifiers Tour, where she bonds with future bestie Kellie Pickler.

MAY 2007

★ At the May 15th Academy of Country Music Awards, Taylor gives a performance to remember, playing her hit "Tim McGraw" for its namesake, and afterward goes up to shake the country legend's hand. She's nominated for Top Female Vocalist, but doesn't win.

JUNE 2007

★ Taylor plays the CMA Country Music Festival, where she discovers her debut album has gone platinum, just eight months after its release! Remembering how far she'd come in such a short time, the performer wrote, "I went the first year as a volunteer (when I was 14) and helped out with getting artists to their radio interviews. Then last year, I was there signing autographs (nobody knew who I was, it was funny) and telling anyone who would listen that I had a single coming out called 'Tim McGraw' and would they please request it at radio . . . haha. Then one year later, there I

was, receiving a platinum plaque for a million copies of my album sold . . . It's been a good year. :-)"

★ While the Brad Paisley Tour is on a break, Taylor joins up for a few shows with Kenny Chesney.

JULY 2007

★ The rising star opens for two of her country music heroes, power couple Tim McGraw and Faith Hill, on their Soul2Soul II tour.

★ *Taylor Swift* hits number one on the Billboard Country Albums chart.

SEPTEMBER 2007

★ While Taylor's all about being personal on her MySpace, she's smart about where to draw the line online, and this month she teams up with Tennessee Governor Phil Bredesen and the Tennessee Association of Chiefs of Police in a public education campaign to help prevent internet crimes against children.

Taylor donated the pink pickup truck her record label gave her for her 18th birthday to the Victory Junction Gang, a camp for sick kids.

OCTOBER 2007

★ On the 16th, just short of a year after her first album, Taylor releases a Christmas EP, *Sounds of the Season: The Taylor Swift Holiday Collection.*

NOVEMBER 2007

★ Even with her recent Christmas release, fans want more Taylor, and so on the 6th, the in-demand singer-songwriter releases a deluxe edition of *Taylor Swift* with four bonus tracks and fun extras like her Grand Ole Opry debut.

★ Though her songs are climbing the charts and her records flying off the shelves, Taylor feels she has actually made it in country music when she is given the Horizon Award from the Country Music Association. It's a moment she still sings about: "It was the night things changed."

DECEMBER 2007

★ Taylor celebrates her 18th birthday on the 13th and gets the best gift ever: her first number one after fans made "Our Song" their own.

★ Taylor rang in a new year full of possibilities on *Dick Clark's New Year's Rockin' Eve.* She had cause for celebration: her debut album was certified double platinum earlier that month.

FEBRUARY 2008

★ Taylor walks the most prestigious of
music's red carpets, attending her first
Grammy ceremony. Nominated for Best
New Artist, she loses to Amy
Winehouse.

★ Though MTV's *TRL* didn't invite a lot
of country artists to come through the
studio, Taylor gets the chance for an
intimate acoustic performance on
February 27.

APRIL 2008

★ At the Miley and Billy Ray Cyrus–hosted CMT Music Awards, Taylor lights up the stage with a performance of "Picture to Burn" and takes home two awards for "Our Song" (Female Video of the Year and Video of the Year). Taylor recalled the moment she won Female Video, writing, "I will never forget the look on my mom's face when they called out my name as the winner of that award. . . . For the first time in my life, I was speechless. I had NO clue winning that was a possibility. I remember just looking out into the crowd and thinking 'How am I this lucky . . . How do I get to live this life . . . ?'"

★ At the untelevised Young Hollywood Awards, Taylor is dubbed Superstar of Tomorrow and awarded a pair of diamond earrings to add a little something to her natural sparkle.

★ *Taylor Swift* goes triple platinum. Taylor marks the occasion with an announcement on April 29 on *Good Morning America* — the same show she appeared on the day of the album's release less than two years earlier.

Taylor and her dad, Scott. Scott loves teasing his daughter. At one award show, Taylor was wearing a gown "made of these giant gold rocks sewn together. Every once in a while, a big chunk would fall off. My dad trailed after me laughing and picking up each piece, going, 'eBay.'"

MAY 2008

★ The theatrical performer makes a splash with her tempestuous performance of "Should've Said No" at the 2008 ACM Awards, and takes home more hardware for Top New Female Vocalist. (She was also nominated for Album of the Year and Top Female Vocalist.)

★ Taylor solidifies her status as teen idol by gracing the cover of *Seventeen*.

★ The star announces a partnership with L.e.i. jeans. The company is a good fit for Taylor who noted, "I love the jeans, and I love what L.e.i. stands for: Life. Energy. Intelligence."

JUNE 2008

★ Taylor returns to *TRL* for a week of co-hosting, starting June 16.

★ Though Taylor missed a lot of the senior year experience, MTV ensures she doesn't miss her senior prom by inviting her to star in an episode of *Once Upon a Prom*, which aired June 21.

JULY 2008

★ To demonstrate her appreciation for all of her team's hard work, Taylor takes her band, crew, and their families to Kona, Hawaii, for a vacation. Taylor blogged, "They've all worked so hard for the past two years without a real break . . . So I took everybody to Hawaii. It's been the most AMAZING week and we all needed it."

★ Taylor releases her limited edition EP *Beautiful Eyes*, which sells 45,000 copies in its first week, taking the number one position on the Billboard Country Chart, with *Taylor Swift* holding the number two spot.

★ Just a month behind her former

Taylor was inspired by Britney Spears' early award-show performances where she would "always do something a little unexpected." Taylor, seen here with the pop idol at the MTV Video Music Awards, has a Britney poster on her wall at home.

classmates, Taylor receives her high-school diploma, graduating from the private Christian school Aaron Academy, which offers a homeschooling program. "Education has always been at the forefront of my priorities, so I'm really glad to have my diploma," Taylor told the Associated Press.

AUGUST 2008

★ With the *Fearless* release approaching, Taylor gets some news to help calm the pre-release jitters — *Taylor Swift* has earned its fourth platinum certification.

★ Remember when those record execs told Taylor there were no young country fans? Taylor proves them wrong with a Teen Choice Award for Choice Breakout Artist.

★ After Cedar Rapids, Iowa, suffered devastating flooding, Taylor announces during a performance that she will donate $100,000 to the Red Cross to help with the flood relief effort. She told *People*, "They've stood by me, they gave me a sold-out show. You've got to pay it forward in life — that's all I did in Cedar Rapids."

SEPTEMBER 2008

★ Taylor jumps across the pond for performances in London (or "Fundon" as Taylor calls it) on the 3rd.

★ Though the song goes "This ain't a fairytale," on September 26, it is the stuff of fairytales when Taylor hears "White Horse" played on one of her favorite TV shows, *Grey's Anatomy*.

★ Taylor is back on the red carpet as MTV's fashion correspondent for the VMAs. The singer is up for Best New Artist, but loses to German rock sensation Tokio Hotel.

OCTOBER 2008

★ Taylor sings the national anthem at game three of the World Series between the Philadelphia Phillies and the Tampa Bay Rays. Aside from years of anthem-singing experience, Taylor got the invite because she used to sing for the minor league Reading Phillies. It is a special moment for Taylor, and for some of the players too, who'd heard a much younger Taylor sing the anthem in their

minor league days, and now they'd all made it to the big leagues!

NOVEMBER 2008

★ On November 8, CMT airs its *Crossroads* special, pairing Taylor with Def Leppard, and proving Taylor's theory that good music breaks through the borders of genre.

★ After a two-year wait for Taylor's sophomore album, *Fearless* drops on November 11. In its first week, the album sells over 10 times the number of copies of Taylor's debut, hitting number one on the Billboard 200. There was no sophomore slump for this unstoppable star.

★ With a new line of dolls from Jakks Pacific, Taylor proves that even in plastic, she's fantastic! The dolls sport Taylor staples like sundresses and sparkly dresses, and even come equipped with her trademark sparkly guitar for composing heartbreak ballads about other dolls. Taylor notes, "I can't wait to see little girls play with my doll and rock out with my crystal guitar."

★ Taylor takes home three BMI Awards for her songwriting, and "Teardrops on My Guitar" is hailed as Country Song of the Year. When Taylor takes the stage to accept her award she gets two thumbs up from Hank Williams Jr. and a text message from Kenny Chesney saying, "Congrats, I love you."

★ Our golden girl gets glammed up for the CMAs, where she reenacts the "Love Story" video (complete with

Taylor with Joe Elliott of Def Leppard. She and her band love Def Leppard, so performing with them was a dream come true: "We were just looking at each other like, 'This is not happening, you've got to be kidding me.'"

Justin Gaston), and is nominated for Female Vocalist of the Year. In the first three years of her career, this is the only CMA Award nomination she doesn't turn into a win.

★ The award-filled month continues when Taylor wins her first American Music Award for Favorite Female Country Artist. The young songstress is overcome with gratitude to her fans for voting for her. She wrote, "I can't tell you how thankful/amazed/excited/ecstatic/over-joyed/blown away I am that you won me my FIRST American Music Award! I've said it before, and I'll say it again now. . . . There's nothing like a fan-voted award."

★ Rumors fly that Taylor is pregnant. She responds on her MySpace blog calling it "the most IMPOSSIBLE thing on the plan-et. Take my word for it. Impossible," and tells *Access Hollywood*, "I didn't do anything to provoke that. Like I'm sit-ting there thinking, like what? Did I wear the wrong shirt?"

★ During her November 11 appearance on *Ellen*, Taylor drops a gossip bomb of her own when she admits that Joe Jonas broke up with her in a 27-second phone call.

DECEMBER 2008

★ Kellie Pickler releases "Best Days of Your Life," a single co-written by Taylor, which ends up staying on the charts for over 40 weeks.

★ On the 23rd, Taylor releases a live album, *iTunes Live from Soho*, that features the songstress performing eight tracks, including a cover of Rihanna's "Umbrella."

★ Taylor celebrates a year of unimaginable success with another performance in Times Square for *Dick Clark's New Year's Rockin' Eve*. The golden girl of 2008 sings a medley of "Should've Said No," "Love Story," "Forever & Always" (with fellow performer Joe Jonas as a captive audience) and "Change." The singer even manages an onstage costume change in a six-minute set, shedding her winter coat to reveal a black, sparkly Stephen Burrows dress. Taylor finishes off the set, like her year, on a high note, telling the crowd, "This is a new year, a new beginning, and things . . . will . . . change!"

★ Taylor is declared *CosmoGirl*'s Girl of the Year for 2008.

JANUARY 2009

★ Taylor makes her first appearance on *Saturday Night Live* as a musical guest. Taylor tells *Glamour*, "I got to meet Kristen Wiig and Andy Samberg, who are some of my favorite people."

FEBRUARY 2009

★ Tickets for the Fearless Tour go on sale and sell out completely minutes later.

★ Though Taylor didn't receive any Grammy noms, she still takes the stage with friend Miley Cyrus to perform "Fifteen."

★ Though she clarifies she's not a designer, Taylor collaborates on a line of

Taylor paints a 13 on her hand before every show; it's her lucky number. "I was born on the 13th. I turned 13 on Friday the 13th. My first album went gold in 13 weeks. My first number-one song had a 13-second intro. Every time I've won an award I've been seated in either the 13th seat, the 13th row, the 13th section or row M, which is the 13th letter. Basically whenever a 13 comes up in my life, it's a good thing."

L.e.i. sundresses available exclusively at Walmart, sharing her signature style with girls everywhere. Always mindful of her audience, Taylor keeps the price to $14, noting, "I never want to put my name on something that an 18-year-old girl struggling through her freshman year of college can't afford, or a family of four who won't spend $150 for a dress."

- ★ Taylor goes on a nine-day promotional tour in England, Scotland, and Germany.
- ★ *Jonas Brothers: The 3D Concert Experience* hits theaters nationwide, with Taylor joining the brothers onscreen to perform "Should've Said No."

MARCH 2009

- ★ The golden-haired beauty is given every musician's dream, a cover of *Rolling Stone.*
- ★ Taylor makes her acting debut on *CSI* on the March 5 episode, "Turn, Turn, Turn." The episode also features a remixed version of "You're Not Sorry."
- ★ *Rolling Stone* names Taylor one of the 100 people who are changing America. But ever-modest Taylor points out to Jay Leno that she was among scientists, neurosurgeons, and environmentalists and under their names they have "all these really technologically profound quotes about the essence of humanity." She adds, "And then you get to mine and it says Taylor Swift, quote: 'Today me and Miley ate a whole pizza in like five minutes!'"
- ★ On March 20, Taylor plays the Houston Rodeo to a massive crowd of 72,658 (the eighth largest crowd ever, outdoing even the Jonas Brothers by 183 people).
- ★ The soundtrack for *Hannah Montana: The Movie* is released on the 24th, which features Taylor Swift's "Crazier," a song she performs in the movie. When the filmmakers emailed her looking for "a song you could fall in love to," Taylor sent them "Crazier," and they fell in love with it. The song peaks at number 17 on the Hot 100 in May, and reaches number 28 on the Pop 100.

APRIL 2009

- ★ At the Academy of Country Music Awards, Taylor wins two major awards, Album of the Year and the Crystal Milestone Award for selling more albums than anyone else that year. Astonished, Taylor remarks, "I write songs in my bedroom, and have so much fun doing this, it doesn't really feel like work. The fact that you can win Album of the Year for that was just unbelievable to me."
- ★ *Forbes* magazine gives Taylor the number four spot on their annual list of country music's top earners, estimating her annual take to be $18 million. She's also the highest-ranked female performer on the list.
- ★ In a major milestone moment, Taylor kicks off her first headlining tour on April 23 in Evansville, Indiana, where that date is declared Taylor Swift Day.
- ★ On the 27th, Taylor goes to class, Journalism 101, with her best friend Abigail at Kansas University. The superstar's presence doesn't go unnoticed. "It's funny how over the course of, like, an hour class that literally one text message can set off a whole campus," said Abigail of the insta-crowd.

MAY 2009

- ★ "Fifteen" inspires a partnership with Best Buy called "@15." @15 is a "teen-led social change platform" that lets teens decide where Best Buy's charitable donations should go. @15 is the official charitable partner of the Fearless Tour, and Taylor recorded a "Teen Service Announcement" that plays at each stop on her North American tour. Before each show, Taylor donates 40 free tickets and an autographed Taylor guitar to teen-focused charities like the YMCA, the Boys and Girls club, and Big Brothers/Big Sisters.

★ On the 31st, Taylor's *Dateline* special airs.

The show goes behind the scenes in the lead-up to the Fearless Tour's launch, revealing a grounded, hard-working young woman, unanimously adored by friends, coworkers, and fans.

JUNE 2009

★ Proving she can rap like the best of the shorties in extra-small white Ts, Taylor films a segment for the CMT Music Awards with T-Pain, poking fun at her good-girl persona in "Thug Story."

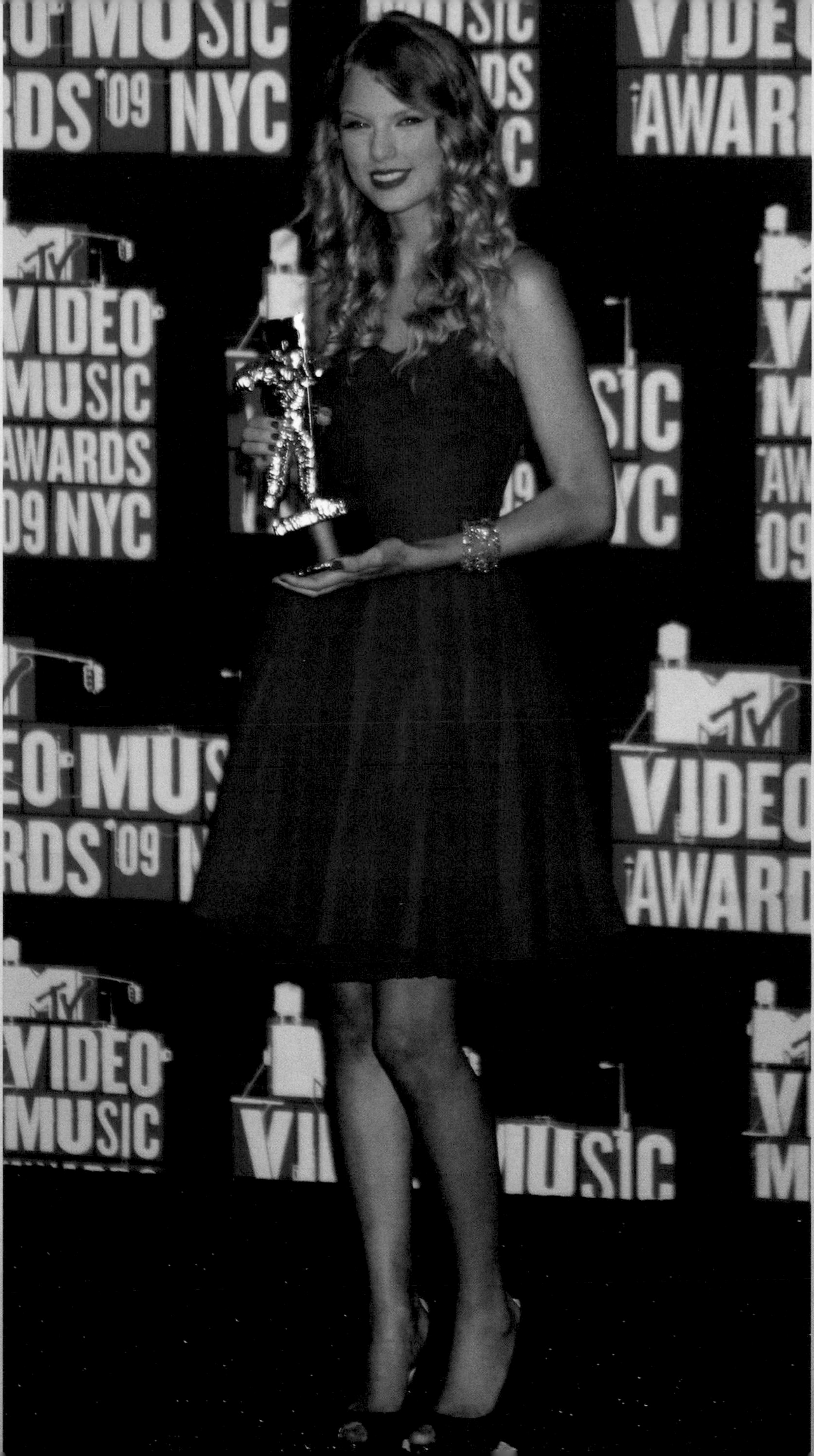
MTV
VIDEO
MUSIC
AWARDS
09 NYC

On September 13, 2009, Taylor was once again defying expectations as a country singer when she took to the stage to accept an MTV Video Music Award for her "You Belong with Me" video. But what happened next was even more unexpected. Just as she started her acceptance speech, rapper Kanye West stormed the stage, grabbing the mic from the astonished singer. He said, "Yo, Taylor, I'm really happy for you, I'll let you finish, but Beyoncé had one of the best videos of all time. One of the best videos of all time!" The camera cut to a shocked and appalled Beyoncé. When Kanye returned the microphone, Taylor stood there stunned and the audience gave her a supportive standing ovation. Sources at the VMAs reported that the 19-year-old burst into tears backstage. At the end of the night, when Beyoncé accepted her award for Video of the Year, she generously invited Taylor up on stage with her to give her the moment that had been stolen from her.

After the ceremony, Kanye's actions came under fire from everyone from average people to celebrities like Pink, Joel Madden of Good Charlotte, Perez Hilton, Katy Perry, and even President Barack Obama. Said Taylor, "I didn't expect anything like that could ever happen and I also didn't expect the support and love that came afterward." Later, Kanye posted a rambling apology on his blog, which was eventually replaced by a more humble admission: "That was Taylor's moment and I had no right in any way to take it from her." Though Kanye apologized publicly on *The Jay Leno Show*, it wasn't until Taylor's appearance on *The View*, that Kanye called personally to apologize. Taylor accepted the apology, and at least there was one consolation — it made for great material in her *Saturday Night Live* monologue.

★ At the CMT Music Awards ceremony, Taylor wins the fan-voted Video of the Year and Female Video of the Year awards. She writes to her fans to thank them in "A driving-home-wondering-how-on-earth-you-got-so-lucky-and-semi-questioning-whether-you-just-hallucinated-the-whole-night kind of way."

AUGUST 2009

★ Taylor surfs to victory with teen voters, earning Teen Choice Awards for Choice Female Album and Choice Female Artist.

★ On August 27, Taylor plays her sold-out-in-one-minute show at Madison Square Garden, and afterward tweets, "Most. Amazing. Night. That's what I'll look back on when I'm old."

OCTOBER 2009

★ After filming some romantic scenes over the summer with Twilight heartthrob Taylor Lautner for *Valentine's Day*, rumors start to really heat up about a Taylor and Taylor power pairing when the two are spotted hanging out. Neither Taylor officially confirms a relationship.

★ Tickets for the 2010 leg of the Fearless Tour go on sale on October 23, and 15 shows sell out within minutes.

★ On October 26, a day before the album's scheduled on-sale date, Taylor releases what she jokingly calls the "Fearless Jedi Ninja Platinum Edition," otherwise known as *Fearless: Platinum Edition*. It doesn't come with Wookies or

nunchucks, but it does come with six new tracks, her videos, behind-the-scenes featurettes, and great photos by her brother Austin. He was invited to be the tour photographer after getting a new camera and snapping some stunning pics.

★ Taylor receives some love from her hometown at the Nashville Music Awards when she's named Artist of the Year, Songwriter/Artist of the Year, and awarded Album of the Year for *Fearless*.

NOVEMBER 2009

★ With the release of *Band Hero* on the 3rd, anyone can try their hand at being Taylor. Taylor is featured in the *Band Hero* commercial with musicians she admires: Travis Barker, Pete Wentz, and Rivers Cuomo.

★ On November 5, Taylor Guitars releases a Taylor Swift guitar that's three-quarter sized, and has vines and the songstress's signature around the sound hole. The guitar reminds the singer of her early days on the road. "I used to sit in the back seat of the rental car while I was on my radio tour at 16, writing songs on my Baby Taylor guitar," said Taylor. "I love the sound, and I love those memories."

★ Taylor makes her return to *Saturday Night Live* on the 7th, this time as host and musical guest. The young star is the first country singer to host the show since one of her idols, Dolly Parton, in 1989.

★ On John Mayer's album *Battle Studies*, Taylor sings on the track "Half of My

Taylor sings her monologue song on *Saturday Night Live* with Bill Hader (left) and Jason Sudeikis (right) making sure she doesn't get Kanye'd again.

Heart." A long-time fan of Mayer's music, Taylor was excited "about just the idea that he would even mention me in his Twitter," let alone that she'd sing a duet with him.

★ Exactly one year after she released *Fearless*, Taylor Swift has another night to remember, when she not only earns Album of the Year at the Country Music Association Awards for her sophomore effort, but also makes history as the youngest person to win the prestigious Entertainer of the Year award. That night, Taylor sweeps her nominations, turning all five into coveted crystal statuettes.

- At the American Music Awards on the 22nd, Taylor wins Artist of the Year. Though Taylor only appears at the awards via satellite from London, she earns five AMAs by the end of the evening.
- Live on British television, Taylor donates £13,000 to Children in Need.
- Though country music is a hard sell overseas, on November 23, Taylor plays for 12,500 British fans at London's Wembley Arena, where, the *Telegraph* noted, "she reinforced her status as every young girl's best friend." Taylor follows with a second show in Manchester on November 24.

DECEMBER 2009

- To celebrate turning the big 2-0 and another year of unimaginable achievement, Taylor throws herself a Christmas-themed birthday party with her friends, band, and tour crew at her home in Hendersonville. This year the songwriter *gives* gifts on her birthday instead of just receiving them — she donates $250,000 to the various schools she attended. "Something I wanted to do at the end of this amazing year and especially on my birthday was give back to something I really believe in, which is education," she said. "The schools that I went to and the amazing people I got to learn from really turned me into who I am, and I wanted to give back."
- Taylor performs at the Z100 Jingle Ball in NYC with other musical sensations like Ke$ha, John Mayer, Justin Bieber,

and Jordin Sparks. Taylor tweeted about the night: "Tonight was one of those nights you don't ever forget the details of. Every little thing was shiny. Jingle Ball. What a way to end the year."
- After a year of unprecedented success, Taylor is the cover girl for *People*'s 25 most intriguing people of 2009 issue. Her company on the list includes Brad Pitt and Angelina Jolie, Sandra Bullock, Neil Patrick Harris, Barack and Michelle Obama, Rihanna, and Sarah Palin.
- Following in the footsteps of Stephen Colbert and Tina Fey, Taylor is named AP Entertainer of the Year. "I am so honored and excited," says Taylor. "This was so unexpected, and I could not be more grateful." Other end-of-the-year honors include being named MTV News' number two Woman of the Year and *Billboard*'s Artist of the Year, with its editors praising her as "a graceful, timeless celebrity" on a swift ascent to the top.

JANUARY 2010

- Once again, the Taylor Nation shows support for their cherished singer-songwriter, and Taylor takes home the People's Choice Award for Favorite Female Artist.
- Just 10 days after a devastating earthquake struck Haiti on January 12, Taylor joins an all-star roster for the Hope for Haiti Now global benefit, donating her time to answer phones, as well as performing a cover of Better Than Ezra's "Breathless." "I've never

Taylor and Faith Hill at a charity event for the Entertainment Industry Foundation's Women's Cancer Research Fund.

actually worked a phone bank before," Taylor said. "But I want to do everything I can to help out this horrible situation. I'm passionate about this. This one was an immediate yes." A recording of her performance was made available on iTunes, with all proceeds going to non-profit associations working in Haiti.

★ On the 19th, Taylor releases "Today Was a Fairytale" for digital download, and it debuts at number two on the Billboard Hot 100, making it her highest debut ever. It has 325,000 downloads in its first week alone, breaking the record for first week sales by a female artist previously held by Britney Spears for "Womanizer."

★ Nashville's princess becomes the Queen of iPods as the highest-selling digital artist in history with 24.3 million downloads.

★ On the 31st, Taylor performs at the Grammy Awards with rock legend Stevie Nicks. Her performance that night comes under fire from the media, but Taylor still has reason to walk away standing tall with four Grammys — Best Country Vocal Performance, Best Country Song, Best Country Album, and Album of the Year.

As Andrea Swift (right) looks on, Liz Rose embraces Taylor as she reacts to winning her very first Grammy.

FEBRUARY 2010

★ On February 12, Taylor makes her acting debut on the silver screen in the ensemble romantic comedy *Valentine's Day*.

★ Just in time for Valentine's Day, Taylor's line of 12 greeting cards with American Greetings is officially available in stores. "Taylor's songs touch millions of people and we believe her cards will have the same emotional appeal . . . we are very excited for everyone to experience them," said American Greetings exec Kelly Ricker.

★ Taylor is nominated for two 2010 Kids' Choice Awards — Favorite Female Singer and Favorite Song for "You Belong with Me."

MARCH 2010

★ Taylor is nominated for four major ACM Awards — Top Female Vocalist, Video of the Year and Song of the Year (for "You Belong with Me"), and Entertainer of the Year.

★ Big Machine releases a free Taylor Swift iPhone application, so "any time Taylor releases new music, videos, or photos (and more), fans will be instantly updated directly on their iPhones."

APRIL 2010

★ Taylor graces the cover of *Elle*'s April issue not just once but twice. One cover features Taylor in a black leather jacket; the other in a signature silver sparkly dress. Says Taylor in the interview, "I like to categorize the various levels of heartbreak. I've only had that happen once. A letdown is worth a few songs. A heartbreak is worth a few albums."

★ At the ACM Awards on the 18th, Taylor performs "Change," and changes her costume halfway through the song. For the rousing finish, Taylor is accompanied by the Tritones, an a cappella group from the University of California, San Diego, then dives into the crowd!

★ Taylor announces that she'll be the newest easy, breezy, beautiful CoverGirl, with a cosmetics campaign debuting in January 2011. Also in April, Taylor's ads for the Sony CyberShot Camera air.

MAY 2010

★ Taylor is part of the all-star ACM concert special *Brooks & Dunn: The Last Rodeo* on the 23rd, with musical guests such as Keith Urban, Carrie Underwood, Reba McEntire, Rascal Flatts, and Brad Paisley.

★ Taylor donates $500,000 to Nashville flood relief. "Being at home during the storm, I honestly could not believe what was happening to the city and the people I love so dearly," Taylor wrote in an email. "Nashville is my home, and the reason why I get to do what I love. I have always been proud to be a Nashvillian, but especially now, seeing the love that runs through this city when there are people in crisis."

★ In the May issue of *Vogue*, Taylor talks about how unbelievable her life is: "Looking back on what these past two years have been for me, it feels like this magical dream of 'Really? We toured all over the world? We played an arena in London? This is happening?' Readjusting my goals and dreams has been something I've had to do a lot lately."

Photo Notes & Credits

Front Cover Performing at a benefit concert for the Red Cross Victorian Bushfire Appeal in Sydney, Australia, on Mar. 14, 2009. (Daniel Boud/Retna)

p. 1 At the Candies Foundation Annual Event to Prevent benefit on May 7, 2008. (Eckstein/Retna Digital)

p. 2 Taylor photographed in 1994. (Andrew Orth/Retna)

p. 5 Taylor, age 11, with Berks Youth Theatre's Cody Derespina, Chris Brossman, and Jessica Flamholz in Mar. 2001. (Diane Staskowski, The Reading Eagle)

p. 6 Taylor's photo was in her local paper after she won a statewide poetry contest. (The Reading Eagle)

p. 8, 11 Taylor in 2004. Note the "I Heart ?" on her hand on p. 8. (Andrew Orth/Retna)

p. 13 In Nashville on Apr. 10, 2006. (John Shearer/WireImage/Getty Images)

p. 14 Leaving Wyomissing for Nashville. (The Reading Eagle)

p. 17 Photographed on May 2, 2000. (Reed Saxon/AP Photo)

p. 20 At the 52nd Annual Grammy Awards pre-telecast show. (Kevin Winter/Getty Images)

p. 23 Backstage at the 44th Annual ACMs on Apr. 5, 2009. (Frazer Harrison/ACM2009/Getty Images)

p. 25 In Nashville on Oct. 19, 2006. (Mark Humphrey/AP Photo)

p. 26 At the 44th Annual ACMs on Apr. 5, 2009. (Jae C. Hong/AP Photo)

p. 28 At a taping for Fox News on Oct. 25, 2006. (Michael Simon/startraksphoto.com)

p. 29 At The Morning Show with Mike and Juliet on Mar. 13, 2007. (Bill Davila/startraksphoto.com)

p. 31 In L.A. on Nov. 5, 2008. (Damian Dovarganes/AP Photo)

p. 33 At the 42nd Annual ACMs. (Mark J. Terrill/AP Photo)

p. 35 At the 41st ACMs on May 23, 2006. (Jacob Andrzejczak/Shooting Star)

p. 37 At the 41st CMA nominations on Aug. 30, 2007. (Barry McCloud/Shooting Star)

p. 41 Performing "Should've Said No" on May 18, 2008. (Mark J. Terrill/AP Photo)

p. 42 Arriving at the 40th Annual CMAs on Nov. 6, 2006. (Chitose Suzuki/AP Photo)

p. 44 Collecting toys for charity on NBC's Today on Nov. 18, 2007. (Ali Paige Goldstein/NBC NewsWire via AP Images)

p. 45 Performing in Atlanta on Sep. 20, 2007. (Robb D. Cohen/Retna)

p. 46 Performing near her hometown. (Susan L. Angstadt, The Reading Eagle)

p. 47 At the 44th Annual ACMs on Apr. 5, 2009. (Dan Steinberg/AP Photo)

p. 48 Opening the 44th Annual ACMs. (Mark J. Terrill/AP Photo)

p. 50 Performing in Kansas City on May 11, 2007. (Jason Squires/WireImage/Getty Images)

p. 51 Arriving at the CMT Music Awards on Apr. 16, 2007. (Jason Moore/ZUMA Press/Keystone)

p. 52 Holding the Horizon Award at the 41st Annual CMAs on Nov. 7, 2007. (Peter Kramer/AP Photo)

p. 55 Performing at Stagecoach 2008 in Indio, CA, on May 3. (Jackie Butler/Retna)

p. 56 Performing on Today on May 29, 2009. (PseudoImage/Shooting Star)

p. 57 At her hometown Walmart in Hendersonville on Nov. 11, 2008. (Aaron Crisler/Retna)

p. 59 Performing during Country Thunder in Twin Lakes, WI, on Jul. 16, 2009. (Rob Grabowski/Retna)

p. 61 After Taylor and Miley's performance of "Fifteen." (John Shearer/WireImage/Getty Images)

p. 63 Performing at the 42nd Annual CMAs on Nov. 12, 2008. (Mark Humphrey/AP Photo)

p. 64 At a pre-Grammy party on Feb. 8, 2008. (Tony DiMaio/Shooting Star)

p. 69 At the Beverly Wilshire Hotel. (Sara De Boer/Retna)

p. 73 Joe Jonas and Taylor sing "Should've Said No" on Jul. 14, 2008, in Anaheim, CA. (Shelby Casanova)

p. 75 At the Sprint Sound & Speed event on Jan. 9, 2010. (Randi Radcliff/AdMedia/Keystone Press)

p. 77 Arriving at the 2008 MTV VMAs on Sep. 7, 2008. (Sthanlee B. Mirador/Shooting Star)

p. 79 In the pressroom at the 2007 CMT Music Awards. (Tammie Arroyo/AP Photo)

p. 80 Backstage on Apr. 14, 2008. (Rick Diamond/WireImage/Getty Images)

p. 82 Performing on Nov. 12, 2008. (ZUMAPRESS.com/Keystone Press)

p. 84 Lucas Till in Apr. 2009. (Albert Michael/startracksphoto.com)

p. 85 Taylor and Andrea Swift arriving at the 42nd Annual ACMs on May 15, 2007. (Charles Santiago/Shooting Star)

p. 87 Performing at Madison Square Garden on Aug. 27, 2009. (Stephen Chernin/AP Photo)

p. 89, p. 90 (top row), **91** (bottom right) The Fearless Tour in Lafayette, LA, on Sep. 10, 2009. (Mallory Bartow)

p. 90 (bottom three), **91** (all but bottom right), **92** The Fearless Tour in Indianapolis, IN, on Oct. 8, 2009. (Adam W. Lewis)

p. 95 At the CMA Awards on Nov. 11, 2009. (Sanford Myers/The Tennessean/ZUMApress.com/Keystone Press)

p. 99 The Fearless Tour in Orlando, FL, on Mar. 5, 2010. (MavrixPhoto.com/Keystone Press)

p. 101 At the *Hannah Montana: The Movie* premiere on Apr. 2, 2009. (Sthanlee B. Mirador/Shooting Star)

p. 102 Nick, Taylor Swift, Joe, and Kevin Jonas in *Jonas Brothers: The 3D Concert Experience.* (Frank Masi, Disney Enterprises, Inc./Fotos International/Keystone Press)

p. 103 With Demi Lovato at the *Hannah Montana: The Movie* premiere. (Matt Sayles/AP Photo)

p. 105 Carrie Underwood, Kelly Pickler, and Taylor at a Nashville Predators game on Dec. 27, 2007. (Mike Strasinger/AdMedia/Keystone Press)

p. 106 Filming in West L.A. on Jul. 30, 2009. (Fame Pictures, Inc./Keystone Press)

p. 107 Waiting to answer phones during the Hope for Haiti Now telethon in L.A. (MTV/Retna)

p. 109 Performing at the Jan. 12, 2008, Sprint Sound & Speed event. (Dan Harr/Shooting Star)

p. 110 A close-up of Taylor's signature boots taken at Pacific Amphitheatre in Costa Mesa, CA, on Jul. 31, 2007. (Kelly A. Swift/Retna)

p. 111 At a *Hannah Montana: The Movie* screening in Nashville on Apr. 9, 2009. (Aaron Crisler/Retna)

p. 113 Performing at KIIS FM's Jingle Ball in L.A. on Dec. 5, 2009. (Christina Radish)

p. 115 Arriving at the MTV VMAs on Sep. 13, 2009. (Christina Radish)

p. 116 At the Clive Davis Annual pre-Grammy gala on Jan. 30, 2010. (Sthanlee B. Mirador/Shooting Star)

p. 119 Arriving at the 2009 CMT Music Awards on Jun. 16. (Bill Davila/startraksphoto.com)

p. 121 Posing with her awards backstage at the 44th Annual ACMs on Apr. 5, 2009. (Jae C. Hong/AP Photo)

p. 122 Posing with her Grammys on Jan. 31, 2010. (Vince Bucci/PictureGroup/AP Images)

p. 124 Performing with Caitlin in Atlanta, GA, on Sep. 3, 2009. (James Palmer/Retna)

p. 126 In London, England, on Aug. 24, 2009. (wenn.com/Keystone Press)

p. 128 At the 40th CMAs on Nov. 6, 2006. (Barry McCloud/Shooting Star)

p. 129 At the Reading Phillies opening game on Apr. 5, 2007. (Krissy Krummenacker, The Reading Eagle)

p. 130 Performing at the Jan. 12, 2008, Sprint Sound & Speed event. (Dan Harr/Shooting Star)

p. 131 Pictured with NASCAR driver Kyle Petty, co-founder of Victory Junction Gang charity. (Dan Harr/Shooting Star)

p. 132 Performing on *Today* on May 29, 2009. (PseudoImage/Shooting Star)

p. 133 At the 2008 CMT Music Awards on Apr. 14. (Curtis Hilbun/AP Photo)

p. 134 At a CMT taping on Oct. 30, 2008. (Rick Diamond/WireImage for CMT/Getty Images)

p. 135 In L.A. on Sep. 7, 2008. (Matt Sayles/AP Photo)

p. 137 Performing at the CMT Music Awards on Jun. 16, 2009. (Mark Humphrey/AP Photo)

p. 138 Miley and Taylor at the premiere of *Hannah Montana: The Movie.* (Matt Sayles/AP Photo)

p. 140 The Fearless Tour in Tampa, FL, on Mar. 4, 2010. (Luis Santana/Times/ZUMApress.com/Keystone Press)

p. 142 In the NYC subway during her VMA performance on Sep. 13, 2009. (Scott Gries/PictureGroup/AP Photos)

p. 143 With her Best Female Video award at the 2009 MTV VMAs. (Christina Radish)

p. 144 Kanye West takes the microphone from Taylor as she accepts her VMA. (Jason DeCrow, file/AP Photo)

p. 146 On *SNL*, Nov. 7, 2009. (Dana Edelson/NBCU Photo Bank via AP Images)

p. 148 In Beverly Hills on Jan. 27, 2010. (ML Agency)

p. 149 Winning a Grammy on Jan. 31, 2010. (Matt Sayles/AP Photo)

p. 150 With her People's Choice Favorite Female Artist award on Jan. 6, 2010. (Christina Radish)

p. 151 Performing at the 43rd Annual CMAs on Nov. 11, 2009, before an audience full of Hendersonville High School students. (Josh Anderson/AP Photo)

p. 153 Performing a sold-out show at Madison Square Garden on Aug. 27, 2009. (Theo Wargo/WireImage for New York Post/Getty Images)

Back Cover At the ACM Awards on Apr. 18, 2010. (Dan Steinberg/AP Photo)

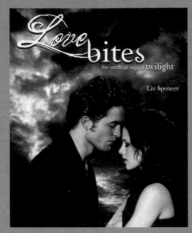

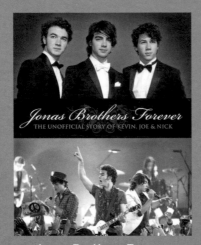

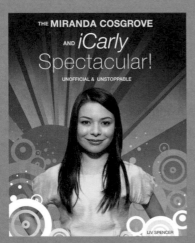